U.S. Catholic Seminaries and Their Future

**Conference Proceedings
January 1988**

Sponsored by
Foundations and Donors Interested in Catholic Activities, Inc.

In Association with
The Lilly Endowment, Inc.

FADICA
Foundations and Donors
Interested in
Catholic Activities, Inc.

Organized in 1976, FADICA is an effort among a growing number of private foundations and donors across the country and in Europe to establish contact and maintain communication with one another. In addition to facilitating the exchange of information among its members, FADICA serves as a forum for the discussion of common grant requests and programs of mutual interest, as a means of coordinating joint efforts by member foundations, and as a way to keep members abreast of recent developments in the Church.

Cover Illustration: Jane Ibrahim
Graves Fowler & Associates; Silver Spring, Md.
Typeface: Melior
Typography: World Composition Services, Sterling, Virginia

ISBN 1-55586-202-0

Contents

Preface

The high velocity of change occurring in Roman Catholic life in the United States is nowhere more evident than in the institution of the seminary. It is a very different enterprise than it was just two decades ago. The seminary of the 1960s, with the stress it placed upon the observance of strict rules, has been replaced today by an institution laying emphasis on maturation, personal autonomy, and developing a sense of responsibility in candidates for the priesthood.

While youth once characterized seminary life, now a greater number of older men are represented among the student body of these institutions, with nearly one-third of all seminarians being thirty-one years of age or older. Further evidence of change can be seen in the fact that only a little more than half of the students in the nation's fifty-four Catholic theologates are studying for the priesthood. The remainder of those enrolled are mostly pursuing studies leading to some form of lay ministry. Filled to capacity in the 1960s, many seminaries now have closed their doors or are sparsely populated, with underutilized faculties and rapidly rising operating costs.

It is to be expected that the future of these schools has become the subject of much debate—a debate influenced by distinctly different views of what comprises the nature of the priestly ministry today. Should seminaries foster a kind of formation environment detached from the world and the rapidly changing context for Catholic ministry? Will these institutions play a central role in preparing laity for service within the Church in the years ahead? With the decline of vocations, who will staff Catholic seminaries, and how will the Church manage to finance these increasingly costly resources?

Those questions and more were explored by church leaders, researchers, seminary rectors, and grant makers during a two-day conference, cosponsored by FADICA and The Lilly Endowment. The meeting sought to touch upon current research relevant to contemporary trends in seminary education and to assist foundations and donors in determining where their resources may be of strategic value to seminary education in the years ahead. This present publication, *U.S. Catholic Seminaries and Their Future*, is the fruition of that conference.

Dr. Francis J. Butler
President
FADICA

WELCOME

Dr. Francis J. Butler

**President
Foundations and Donors
Interested in
Catholic Activities, Inc.**

INTRODUCTION

Mr. Fred L. Hofheinz

**Program Director, Religion
The Lilly Endowment, Inc.**

DR. BUTLER: On behalf of the Board of Directors of FADICA, it is a pleasure to extend a welcome to each of you.

The Catholic seminary. In the popular mind, the term conjures up prosaic images of Gothic-style buildings situated in rural settings, the ringing of Angelus bells, and young men diligently attentive to their priest professors of moral theology. The reality these days may be something quite different. When we speak of the seminary, no *one* image seems to apply.

Education for the priesthood can take place in freestanding institutions, like the one described; in a union; in a university-related organization; in a cluster of theological schools; in a federation; as well as in a number of other variations.

Students may be young, but probably are not. They may be listening to a priest professor or a lay person. And chances are, they may not be the only students in the room.

Many of us in FADICA almost certainly will come away from this discussion with a revised understanding of what seminary education looks like today, as well as the changes projected for its future. This is as it should be, for the choice of this topic has been based upon FADICA's desire to understand these institutions better. They are a most important part of the Church's life, yet historically, perhaps by virtue of the way they have been financed—principally through diocesan seminary burses—seminaries have been somewhat remote from the range of Catholic foundation work. I know that some of you hope to change that while you are here!

Over the past dozen years, FADICA has studied a host of issues from vocations to the priesthood and religious life, to new and emerging lay ministries. Nearly all of these discussions share a common thread: they anticipate the Church's future, and they direct energy, thinking, and intellectual resources where they will help foundations and donors prepare for that future.

This series of exchanges has been beneficial to the funding programs of our members, but these exchanges have also had a catalytic impact on the broader Church, to whom the proceedings of this gathering will be made available.

We are delighted to co-sponsor today's meeting with the Lilly Endowment, which has singularly distinguished itself over the years by its abundant support and enhancement of Catholic seminary education. It is a pleasure to introduce to you our co-host and this afternoon's symposium facilitator, a man who is perhaps most responsible for today's gathering, Mr. Fred Hofheinz of the Lilly Endowment.

MR. HOFHEINZ: I do want to join Dr. Butler in welcoming all of you to this FADICA Conference on U.S. Catholic Seminaries. I have looked forward to this gathering for a long, long time, for it represents an exceptionally important moment for the work of the Lilly Endowment and for me personally.

As I look back on my fifteen-year career as a staff officer at the Endowment, I count my work with and for the Catholic seminary enterprise as among the more important contributions that this foundation has made to the understanding of religion in American life. Though I want to be careful not to overstate this, I have a feeling that Lilly-sponsored studies of the Catholic seminary and Catholic ministry have made a major impact on the planning and thinking of decision makers in the American Church during the 1980s and will continue to influence those decision makers well through the end of this century.

As I have mentioned from time to time at other FADICA gatherings, we at the Lilly Endowment are fond of likening our grants for religious research to a kind of "early warning system" which can help illumine the landscape of things to come.

Through our research grants, we hope to highlight today's critical issues with an eye toward aiding leaders in the Church—lay and clergy alike— as they attempt to make the kinds of decisions that will shape the Church of the future. As Catholic University sociologist Dean Hoge says in his recently published Lilly-sponsored book, *Future of Catholic Leadership:* "Where the Church should go is a theological question to be decided in prayer and study by Catholic leaders. The role of research is merely to provide information and interpretation of current conditions."

Leadership in the Church or in any other enterprise is difficult enough as it is, but it is nearly impossible in today's world without adequate and accurate information. The trick for a foundation that wants to help in this, of course, is to choose correctly from among the wide range of issues that merit exploration. Our decision at Lilly to concentrate much of our Catholic research on theological seminaries and the future of ministry has turned out to have been a providential one. It came both from historical reality—the Endowment's strong interest in theological education—and from a reading by our staff of what Vatican II has rightly called "The signs of the times."

We began grants for research about Catholic seminaries in 1979 with our support of the first-ever national study of the financing of Catholic theological education, the so-called CARA/LILLY Report. And since that time, we have invested well over a million dollars on this issue. We have never doubted the rightness of our decision to concentrate on this theme. But the wisdom of that decision really came home to me when I read some of the remarks that the Holy Father made when addressing the American bishops last September in Los Angeles, at which time he said, quite simply: "The Church of tomorrow passes through the seminaries of today." This has been a constant theme of Pope John Paul II from the earliest days of his pontificate: seminaries are the key to church renewal.

Last June, the English edition of *L'Osservatore Romano* printed a speech that the Holy Father had made in Germany at the dedication of a new seminary, in which he said: "The Second Vatican Council stated that all priests should regard the seminary as 'the very heart of the diocese.' The way that heart beats has a determining long-term effect on religious and church life out in the parishes. That is why seminaries are of key importance."

I am very pleased that you, my FADICA colleagues, have invited us to share the fruits of some of our learning about the American seminary with you. I count you as among the leaders of the American Catholic Church, and I have long coveted this opportunity to help open up for you some of the rich learning about the present and the future of this enterprise, which is coming into focus through the Endowment's grant making.

Though we could not begin to range across the entire landscape of the Catholic seminary world in these few hours, I trust that you will have the opportunity to begin to become acquainted with this terrain. You will have as your guides during this exploration a sparkling array of speakers and panelists, who represent among them a group of the most knowledgeable men and women in America about this topic. I think you will find these next few hours informative and stimulating.

U.S. CATHOLIC SEMINARIES ANTICIPATING THEIR FUTURE

Speaker

Most Rev. Thomas J. Murphy

Chairman
Bishops' Committee on Priestly Life
and Ministry
National Conference of Catholic Bishops

Facilitator

Mr. Fred L. Hofheinz

Program Director, Religion
The Lilly Endowment, Inc.

MR. HOFHEINZ: There is really no better way to start this gathering than with our keynote speaker. I first met Archbishop Murphy in 1973 when he was the newly appointed rector of St. Mary of the Lake Seminary, Mundelein, the major seminary for the Archdiocese of Chicago, and I was just beginning my years as a foundation executive at Lilly. Now he is an Archbishop and I am still in the same old job.

Archbishop Murphy served as president-rector of St. Mary of the Lake from 1973 to 1978, when he was named bishop of Great Falls-Billings, Montana. Last summer, the Holy Father named him coadjutor archbishop of Seattle.

Archbishop Murphy has dedicated most of his priestly life to the work of seminary formation. His leadership position in the national life of the Church is widely acknowledged and deeply respected. He has been chairman of the NCCB Committee on Priestly Formation and currently is the chairman of the Bishops' Committee on Priestly Life and Ministry. Likewise, he has served as chairman of the Executive Committee of the Seminary Department of the National Catholic Educational Association. As leader of the two major National Assemblies of Rectors and Ordinaries held in 1983 and 1987, he has spent countless hours and traveled thousands of miles preparing for those watershed events.

Simply put, there was no other person in the country better qualified to keynote this gathering than Archbishop Thomas Murphy. No single person has contributed more to the work of priestly formation in the United States over the past ten years than has he. I count it a great personal privilege to introduce to my FADICA colleagues my friend, Archbishop Thomas Murphy.

ARCHBISHOP MURPHY: I am extremely grateful for the invitation to be a part of this gathering of church leaders, researchers, seminary president-rectors, and grant makers as together we explore the future of Roman Catholic seminaries here in the United States of America. This gathering gives me an opportunity also to express personally on my own behalf and on the behalf of countless others in the seminary community our deep gratitude to the Lilly Endowment, Inc. and Foundations and Donors Interested in Catholic Activities, Inc., for the sustained interest in, and commitment to, the ministry and mission of seminary education and formation today. Your support of research, conferences, leadership training, and development has given the Church in the United States an awareness of the dynamics involved in seminary education and formation today that would not have been possible without your help and assistance. Thank you for continuing to share that gift so generously, as is obvious from our gathering here these days to reflect on the future of seminaries in our country.

I find it interesting that my own presentation is expected to address the future, as I am asked to look at U.S. Catholic seminaries and to see if I am able to anticipate that future.

My task is as enviable as a Wall Street analyst's today who might be asked to do the same as far as the stock market would be concerned. Yet, in many ways, that analogy is far from irrelevant. There are certain realities within society and the Church that have an inner strength and stamina, yet these realities must face the future in light of forces that impact on them.

I also find it interesting that my own reflections on the future of U.S. Catholic seminaries precede the summary of research that will be provided us as a result of many studies on every aspect of seminary education and formation. My own reflections precede as well the insights that will be shared with us regarding the identity of the priest and the responsibility for ministerial formation within the Church.

The question, "What is a priest?" is of tremendous significance because when we are able to articulate a theology of priesthood that is appropriated by the Christian community, then we will have a clearer idea of the direction of seminary education and formation today in its task of preparing ordained leaders for the Church of tomorrow. At the same time, we recognize the need for the preparation of qualified lay personnel, who are assuming an ever-increasing role and responsibility in the Church, and we must ask the questions regarding their ministerial formation and education. Such increased roles and responsibilities by laity within the Church are not self-directed, but they come from the challenge of Vatican II, post-Vatican II documents, a theology of baptism, and the real needs of the Christian community.

A consideration of the future as the first contribution to this discussion will be tempered by the experience and expertise of those who have come here to share their presence, their insights, their vision, and their wisdom.

Yet an opportunity to reflect on the future of a subject that has critical importance to us who are gathered here as well as to the Church in general is a distinct privilege. I am able to offer what I believe to be the future of U.S. Catholic seminaries and, if future years prove me correct, then I have helped to shape that future by being able to identify the tensions, forces, and vision that will create that future to which we must respond. If my vision is blurred, then my remarks will be part of that ever-increasing limbo of "what might have been" if they had only listened to me.

Allow me to outline what I hope to share with you. The future is unknown, yet we do know that so many dimensions of the future are determined by present realities. Consequently, I would like first to offer some insights on present realities within the Church as well as within seminary education and formation today. Second, I would like to reflect on forces operating within society and the Church today that are helping to shape not only seminary education and formation, but the Church as well. In light of these realities and the forces that impact on them, one is able to see some possible future directions for seminaries in the United States as we conclude one millennium and begin another. Finally, I would like to offer some personal observations in the light of these realities, forces, and future possibilities.

It seems appropriate that as we anticipate the future of seminaries in the United States, we recall certain realities that are in place, which serve as agenda items that will help determine their future. What would some of those realities be? They would have to include the following:

1. Organizationally, the Church is hierarchical. Though themes of collaboration, shared responsibility, response to local needs, and a host of other theological insights have influenced much of the life of the Church, it has to be recognized that legislation for the governance, purpose, mission, and ministry of a seminary cannot be isolated or independent of the expectations of the universal Church. Canon 242 states that "each nation should have a program for priestly formation which is to be determined by the conference of bishops. . . ." But it goes on to say that this program of priestly formation should be developed "in light of the norms issued by the supreme authority of the Church and which is also to be approved by the Holy See. . . ." Even when new circumstances require the program to be updated, approval of the Holy See is also a requirement.

2. Seminaries after Vatican II responded to the challenge of post-conciliar expectations for the formation and education of its ordained min-

isters. There were innovative and intelligent responses to this challenge of meeting the signs of the times. Different forms and structures began to develop within seminary programs. In trying to utilize the resources of finances and personnel in the best way possible, many seminaries developed into centers for not only the formation and education of priests, but also the formation and education of other ministers. Seminaries began to use the gifts and talents of religious, deacons, and priests as faculty members. In doing so, seminaries believed they were faithful to the broad principles of seminary formation and education articulated in the *Program of Priestly Formation*, which allowed for adaptation and response to local needs.

Yet the recent program of visitations to seminaries called for by the Holy See has raised a new consciousness of the norms for seminary formation and education found not only in the *Program of Priestly Formation*, but also in the universal law and norms of the Church. Significant issues have surfaced in light of the visitation experience that need to be addressed by seminaries.

3. As institutions established for the formation and education of candidates for the priesthood, seminaries are only able to accept male students who are willing to make a lifetime celibate commitment as candidates for holy orders. According to many surveys and recent studies, this is a reality that has had a profound effect in the recruitment of candidates for priesthood as well as being an issue for some women who wish to have a more significant participation in the life, governance, and leadership within the Church.

4. Within seminary education and formation today, there is the growing realization that programs of preparation for priesthood are different for candidates for religious communities than the program of preparation for diocesan candidates. The last edition of the *Program of Priestly Formation*, published in 1981, spoke of one program for both sets of candidates. This was done in direct response to the request of the formation committee of the Conference of Major Superiors of Men. Within a very short time, however, it is obvious that a new dimension in seminary formation and education is occurring.

5. The research from the various studies that have taken place over the past five years would indicate the increasing presence of candidates for priesthood today who are characterized by an older age, different edu-

cational backgrounds, and different interests as far as ministry is concerned. This places new expectations on seminary programs.

6. For various reasons, there seems to be an ebb and flow of enrollment trends among individual theologates. The number of candidates for ordained ministry remains more or less the same, which means the dramatic increase in enrollment in one or more seminaries will involve a decrease in others. Enrollment statistics in individual seminaries are a constant reminder of the good news/bad news adage. Ways must be found to stabilize enrollments in individual seminaries as well as to encourage the recruitment of qualified candidates.

7. Collaboration in ministry with others in service to people in the Church today is an expectation of priests, especially those involved in diocesan and parish ministry. Though opportunities to prepare for such collaboration are present within the seminary program, this will remain an issue that seminaries will continue to address.

8. Last, but far from least, is the need for seminaries to articulate a theology of priesthood that will be a basis for the educational/formational process in seminary programs as well as a basis for future priestly ministry. Church statements, as well as ongoing references by Pope John Paul II, ask us to recognize the difference between the ministry of the ordained priest and the ministry that comes from the baptismal call.

The realities I share with you are but some of the forces and issues in place that need to be considered in any discussion of the future of Catholic seminaries in the United States. To plan for the future without taking these realities into consideration would be unrealistic.

At the same time that these factors are in place that impact directly on seminary education and formation, there are also forces within the Church and society that will influence the seminary of today and tomorrow. Some of these forces would be:

1. The ongoing development and change in the lived experience of ministry in the Church today has been broadened to include an ever increasing number of nonordained persons in service to the Church. These ministers expect and want the professional training and expertise needed for their respective positions. Such training and expertise have become requirements within church structures. The question continues to be asked where and how this training can best take place.

2. The reservoir of degreed, competent, and interested priests, who were once the exclusive components of seminary faculties in all areas of seminary formation and education, is not present to the same extent as it was a few decades ago. This places severe tensions on seminaries that want to offer quality programs in conformity with church norms.

3. The escalating costs of seminary formation and education have become a significant factor in the life of the Church. The cost factor is not only a material one, but also the "person" costs in the time and resources needed to prepare qualified faculty members whose effectiveness is limited because of the relatively few students who are able to benefit from the faculty person.

4. We have witnessed a decline in the number of vocations for priesthood as well as the aging of the clergy presently serving the Church, in addition to the departure of priests from the active ministry. Publicity given to tensions in the Church as well as inappropriate actions of clerics all combine to place new pressures and incredible expectations on seminaries.

5. At the heart of many of the issues impacting on seminary formation and education today is the broader issue of ecclesiology, which touches almost every area of church life. It seems that people have different experiences, understandings, and expectations of the Church, which will then influence the program of preparation of candidates for ministry to serve that Church.

6. Forces within the world that impact on the future of seminaries in the United States can range from new forms of individualism to a new sexual morality, to the materialism that reduces the value of the spiritual and transcendent.

7. A final force, among others, which is having a profound effect on the Church as well as on our country, is the increased and growing presence of Hispanics as members of the Church who ask us to respect and appreciate their language, culture, traditions, and values. A consciousness of the Hispanic presence also demands an awareness of the other growing minority communities within the Church—the blacks, native Americans, and Asians.

These factors within the Church and society do not exhaust the forces bearing on seminary formation and education today, but they do give us some idea of the issues that need to be addressed if seminaries are to fulfill their purpose and mission.

I believe it would be helpful if we could determine what will be asked of the ordained priest in the years ahead. If we know what is expected of him, then we will be able to provide a seminary experience that will meet this reality.

In the fall of 1987, the Bishops' Committee on Priestly Life and Ministry published a book titled *A Shepherd's Care: Reflections on the Changing Role of Pastor* (USCC Office of Publishing and Promotion Services). Though the document has as its primary focus the role of pastor and the changing roles, relationships, and environment that have occurred over the past twenty years in fulfilling the role of pastor, much of what is shared in this book could apply to every priest in any ministry within the Church today.

Chapter 5 of *A Shepherd's Care* speaks of the future in terms of a challenge to continue. It describes trends that will continue to have significant impact on the role of the pastor, and it suggests challenges that need to be considered in face of such realities. The three distinct or interrelated trends that will impact the Church will include the following: (1) the changing profile of the American parish; (2) the changing resources for parish staffing; and (3) the changes in parish status and leadership structures.

I believe it is worth considering what these trends suggest to seminary programs as well as the challenges they offer to pastors. In identifying such trends and challenges, we are offering seminaries an agenda for the future.

1. The first trend is the changing role of the American parish. Population shifts, ethnic changes, a combination of a growing older and younger population, combined with what is described as a "spirit of selective compliance," all come together to offer a unique challenge that will involve evangelization and pastoral service.

How the parish will respond to the challenge of growth or decline will depend so much on the leadership offered. There will be pain as parishes are consolidated in some areas and struggle in others as the Church tries to meet growth and expansion. The parish will be asked to meet especially the needs of the ever-changing ethnic and cultural character of communities as well as an even greater urgency to serve the needs of the growing senior-citizen community.

Pastoral service will continue to be the model for parishes, but there will be a greater need for Catholic forms of evangelization and outreach, especially in service to the Hispanic community and in response to the growing problem of fundamentalism.

Are seminaries today recognizing this trend and preparing candidates to meet this challenge?

2. A second trend is the needed adjustment to the decline of the number of ordained priests available for parish service. The transfer of priests from administrative positions to pastoral assignments, extended service of pastors beyond retirement age, the continued growth of the permanent diaconate, and the increased presence of professional and volunteer lay ministers will become realities in almost every local church in the United States.

The challenge for priests will be the adjustment to an almost exclusively sacramental ministry where the priest is the indispensable and only minister. The priest will be challenged to exercise real ingenuity in forging new relationships that will enhance his relation with deacons and lay ministers, especially women. Pastors must face the practical issues of appropriate compensation systems and job security for nonordained ministers as well as certification processes. Pastors will be asked to help develop a lay ministry spirituality as well as to respond to the needs of lay and family life.

Are seminary programs today recognizing this trend and responding to the challenge that it offers?

3. A third trend will be significant changes in parish status and leadership structures. Some parishes will close; others will become missions; some will be consolidated. The clustering of parishes will become a greater reality, bringing with it the challenge to maintain some distinct identity for the parish community with the consequent reduction or sharing of pastoral services.

Among the many challenges that this trend suggests will be the transformation of people's anger and frustration into energizing sources of new life. Another challenge will be the support and development of people other than priests exercising pastoral supervision of a community.

Are seminary programs today recognizing this trend and responding to the challenge that it offers?

In light of these trends, the question must be asked whether seminary models called for by church laws, norms, and guidelines are able to prepare candidates to be the pastors or priests described in *A Shepherd's Care* and to have the theological competence, spiritual formation, and ministerial skills to be such a pastor or priest in an effective way.

Seminaries in the United States since Vatican II have been, for the most part, very effective in meeting the signs of the times, in responding to the needs of the Church as lived and experienced by people within the Christian community. In many ways, seminaries have been faithful to the challenge of *Evangelii Nuntiandi* in preparing ordained ministers to proclaim the gospel in a relevant way that meets the needs of the place and culture, while remaining faithful to our tradition as a Roman Catholic faith community.

The recommendations, norms, and guidelines that will be articulated by the Congregation for Catholic Education as a result of the total visitation experience will be proposed as the basis for seminary education and formation in the years ahead. Some guidelines have already been shared; others will continue to be offered.

The question must be asked whether a dialogue might take place regarding such norms when, in the minds and experience of some, the purpose and goals of seminary education and formation of future ordained priests might best be achieved in another way. This becomes the key question that will help determine the future of Catholic seminaries in our country. However, in proposing this question, we must also be open to the response given.

The seminary is more than an educational institution or a place for the formation of candidates for priesthood because of its unique collection of students, staff, and faculty, and because of the influence that its sponsoring religious community or diocese has on it. In the reality of church life and experience, the seminary often becomes the lightning rod for tensions, ideas, and trends, as well as holding patterns for what is happening or will happen in the Christian community. Whether in future years that lightning rod can capture and harness the energy that comes from its search to fulfill its mission or whether it becomes a conduit for its own self-destruction will help to determine the future of seminaries in the United States.

In western Washington, we are blessed with countless examples of the beauty of God's creation. Mt. Rainier is one of the best examples of that creation. However, it happens that for many visitors to Seattle, the fog, clouds, and rain prevent people from being able to see Mt. Rainier. Yet the mountain is there with its unique beauty and its symbolic strength as it stands etched against an endless sky. When days are clear—and there really are many such days in Seattle—Mt. Rainier is an incredible sight.

Seminaries in the United States are much like Mt. Rainier. They are often hidden from view by various forces and people who are unable to see the strength and vision they offer. Yet that strength is present as a powerful force and gift to the Church today in preparing candidates to be priests who serve the people of God in the Church of today and tomorrow.

To those responsible for seminary education and formation in the Church today and to those who help make this enterprise possible, thank you for all you share and do. Thank you for listening.

FLOOR DISCUSSION

MR. HOFHEINZ: We will now entertain questions from the floor.

DR. BUTLER: Archbishop, in the past you have addressed your brother bishops about the question of seminary faculties and the dwindling resources, and to some extent you touched on that here. Would you talk about the problem of diocesan, inner-diocesan cooperation in light of the dwindling numbers of available priests, the sharing of priests, and so forth?

ARCHBISHOP MURPHY: I can speak much more from the point of view of diocesan seminaries. I think religious orders are in a different category, but they're still looking for people. I have just begun to hear about dioceses sharing faculty people. The enterprise of seminary education and formation, on the part of the diocese that does not have a resident sender, has to be almost a "corporate enterprise," almost a contractual thing: we send you our students; we will also send you faculty people to be of help and assistance. Second, it gives an advantage to the local Church because there is the presence of someone from that local Church in the wider gathering of people to which the students can relate.

Recently, I again looked at the *ad limina* reports that we're supposed to fill out. The question, "Does your diocese have its own theologate?" is still asked. I remember showing that to the people who fill out that survey in Great Falls-Billings, Montana. Can you imagine a diocese such as ours having its own theologate? And yet that question is still in the report. But what that question has always raised for me is that there is the expectation, which I appreciate, that says the local Church should have involvement in the training and formation of its ordained people. What we do, of course, is sublet that out. But I believe very strongly in a sharing in that. I think we have to be—if we buy into what we say about how important seminaries are—more open to sharing degreed, gifted people who could be in the seminary role.

DR. BUTLER: I have one follow-up question. The pool of available priests is shrinking, especially those who would have an inclination to obtain advanced degrees to teach in the seminaries. Is there some kind of a reluctance to get into seminary formation and education that was not there years ago?

ARCHBISHOP MURPHY: My own perception would be that among diocesen priests—and I am not sure if it would be true of religious as well—there is that reluctance. I think Sr. Schuth would have a great deal of statistical material on this.

I remember back in 1958 being asked to go on for postgraduate work. That was after so many years in the seminary, gearing my whole life toward working with people—not with going to the library again. At the heart of the spirituality of the pastoral ministry is the greatest show on earth: people. And that whole sense of stepping back from that is, I think, probably the hardest thing to do.

Would this same reluctance be true regarding religious? Fr. Brown?

FR. BROWN: I am more in touch with the diocesan side, but from what I hear from other provincials, that would certainly be true. They have a very difficult time getting anyone to go into formation work in general, and then keeping them there more than two or three years is extremely difficult. They experience loneliness and burnout; they don't get a tremendous amount of support.

ARCHBISHOP MURPHY: Sr. Schuth, would you agree?

SR. SCHUTH: Yes, it is very much the case. The encouragement to go on, the time it takes, and the money required for religious orders—those are all issues.

FR. CUSHING: Archbishop, could you speak a little more about the question of dialogue?

ARCHBISHOP MURPHY: I just mentioned *Evangelii Nuntiandi*, which speaks, as you know, of the need to adapt to the local culture and the need for the gospel to be proclaimed in a way that can be assimilated by the people for whom it is shared. If you transfer that to the whole world of seminary education and formation, we recognize the need to have a universal experience as Catholics. But how it takes shape and form in different cultures, different experiences, I think, comes as a result of understanding and appreciating the local situation. And so, my recommendation would be to structure dialogue with the responsible people in a respectful honest way. I think sometimes the stance is taken that we can sit back and be critical without dialogue, but the very nature of the educational and formational enterprise calls for mutual communication.

MR. HOFHEINZ: Archbishop, you mentioned briefly the recent Vatican visitation of the U.S. seminaries. Although the seminary people here are very familiar with that study, I am not sure the FADICA members are. Could you speak a bit about it and tell us what—if anyone knows—will become of it?

ARCHBISHOP MURPHY: For the benefit of those who are not aware of it, it's a study that was requested by our Holy Father, Pope John Paul II, to reflect on the experience of seminaries in the United States and to see how they respond to the guidelines and norms not only of our own *Program of Priestly Formation*, but the norms of the universal Church.

The whole program began about six or seven years ago, and it is now reaching its final stages. A group composed of bishops, religious superiors, priests, and others has visited every seminary on the theologate or college level as well as houses of formation and has tried to reflect with those seminaries on their responses to the goal and purpose of seminary education. Bishop John Marshall is the one who has coordinated all this, and on a regular basis, he meets with the Holy Father and the Congregation for Education.

About two years ago, the "Report on the Free-Standing Seminaries" was issued, which indicated certain insights that the Congregation received from that first set of visitations. And out of that came a set of reminders, expectations, persuasions, and insights, regarding seminary education today.

MR. HOFHEINZ: Msgr. Baumgaertner?

MSGR. BAUMGAERTNER: Archbishop Murphy, my work is one in which I have to deal with a broad range of seminaries not only Catholic but Protestant.

One of the principal concerns across the country when visiting teams go in for the reaffirmation of the accreditation of the schools is what we call "faculty planning." The one thing they always insist on is that a school should have some plan for what falls into the general category of "faculty development." By that they mean not just how often do you give your people sabbaticals but, above all, what kind of a plan do you have for the replacement of people who will retire or who will be going on to do other work. This is done on a five- to ten-year basis.

The unique problem of seminaries is that seminaries are denominationally related and always have to plan in relation to denominational expectations. That complicates the picture: schools are not able to walk into the general market as such; the planning has to be related to church. Could you offer a Roman Catholic perspective on this? I have a feeling that we fell way behind in the 1970s in the area of planning ahead, and we are paying the price for that now. We are not the only ones; I find this in other denominations as well.

ARCHBISHOP MURPHY: Perhaps Sr. Schuth would have some statistics on that. But the one comment I would make is that one of the strongest things to surface from the "Report on Free-Standing Seminaries" is tremendously high praise of the leadership in the faculties of seminaries. And what happens, then, is that a number of those people are chosen for other ministries in the Church: provincials, bishops, and so forth. This has happened time and time again, which is a compliment, I suspect, to the seminaries in many ways. But I can think of a number of people who now have provincial administration positions or have been named bishop, who once were rectors of seminaries. So you have a high turnover. What is the rate of rectors right now? Five, six years?

SR. SCHUTH: In fact, a little bit less. In three years, half of them turned over.

ARCHBISHOP MURPHY: In three years, half the rectors of the fifty-three theologates in our country turned over. You transfer that to the corporate world, and I don't know if that is as rapid a change; I doubt it.

MSGR. BAUMGAERTNER: This is not unusual in the Protestant seminaries. It is very close to that at the present time.

MR. ROBINSON: Archbishop, my impression from reading the Catholic press is that a lot of the young men who are going to seminary today have a certain pastoral style that is out of sync with the realities and the leadership style that are addressed in *A Shepherd's Care*. If that is true, can seminaries change those men so that they are more in step with today's pastoral reality and leadership style?

ARCHBISHOP MURPHY: Good question. First of all, there are definitely some candidates who are not ready to appropriate the required pastoral style. On the other hand, there are a lot who are. I think that is where the "corporate enterprise" of a religious community or a diocese with a seminary is involved. More and more both work together in screening and selecting candidates.

Many people have said that they would be interested in transferring the RCIA process to seminary formation. I suspect what they are talking about would be that first catechumenate stage of how do you get people immersed into that whole sense of what ministry is and what they are preparing for.

The background of the candidate for theologate is far different than that of the candidate of thirty years ago.

A lot of the people who are applying for service as potential ordained candidates, as well as the people applying for ministerial jobs—lay people, religious—are competent, good, gifted people. And I think one of the really superb things that's developing is interest in having admission procedures and processes that will help young people discern whether this is the best choice for them.

FR. BROWN: I was wondering if you might want to comment on the other end of the whole training process, that is, on the kind of postordination education or formation that might be needed. The seminary career can be very short—only four years perhaps—and to try to accomplish all the goals that are in *A Shepherd's Care* would be extremely difficult. I think there is probably a need for ongoing formation.

ARCHBISHOP MURPHY: A committee of the Conference of Bishops of England and Wales is in the first stages of preparing their *Program of Priestly Formation*. I find the direction it takes is fascinating. Let me just share some of that document with you. In the theological preamble, the committee considers the relationship between the common priesthood of the baptized and the ministerial priesthood. It states, "The sacraments of initiation make all Christians participate in Christ's body, the Church. The sacrament of ordination makes some participate also in its headship of that body."

It continues: "The diaconate should be seen as the start of a lifelong stage in postordination formation rather than the end of the preordination stage." The diaconate is the entrance into ordained ministry. Yet, when a person is ordained a deacon, somehow that seems to be the end of his education. It goes on to say: "In the early years, the priesthood should be seen as an apprenticeship. There should be someone in each diocese who is responsible for the continuing formation of newly ordained priests." I am intrigued by the use of the word *formation* instead of *education*. Basically, this document is the committee's report to the bishops of England and Wales. I am not sure if they have accepted it. Fr. Costanzo, would you know?

MSGR. COSTANZO: They have accepted that first document, which is, as you mentioned, a preamble to a *Program of Priestly Formation*. Now they are beginning to work, on the basis of that document, toward doing a program for formation—in contrast to our bishops, who have now had three editions of the program.

ARCHBISHOP MURPHY: The committee devised a similar program in two phases, the first lasting one or two years according to the students' rate of development, which is—in response to Mr. Robinson's insight— more in the nature of a continuing process of development as a committed Christian than a highly specific preparation for ordained ministry.

Again, my basic contention is that when we talk about the future, we have to *really* talk about the future—those unfolding realities within the

Church, within society, and within the world. And that is where your help and support are going to be needed very much. Together, we can help shape that future, which will provide the Church with ministers—ordained and nonordained—in service to the Church in the years ahead.

MR. HOFHEINZ: Archbishop, we are grateful to you. It is a real sign of hope for the American Church that a man of your integrity and ability is taking such a leadership role both in seminaries and now in your capacity as chairman of the NCCB Committee on Priestly Life and Ministry.

AMERICAN SEMINARIES AS RESEARCH FINDS THEM

Speaker

Dr. Katarina Schuth, OSF

Weston School of Theology
Study Coordinator
The Future of Catholic Seminaries

Panel

Rev. Robert Sherry

Executive Director
Bishops' Committee on Priestly Formation
National Conference of Catholic Bishops

Rev. Eugene Hemrick

Director of Research
United States Catholic Conference

Rev. Vincent Cushing, OFM

President
Washington Theological Union

Rev. David Nygren, CM

Boston University

Rev. Charles Froehle

Rector
Saint Paul Seminary

MR. HOFHEINZ: In 1983, the Lilly Endowment published the results of a major five-year study, which had been carried out by an Episcopalian priest and former seminary president, Dr. John Fletcher. This study, entitled *The Futures of Protestant Seminaries,* traced the impact of a number of past and present trends as an aid to leaders who worry about and plan for the future of the theological schools that they serve. Quite early on in his project, Dr. Fletcher decided to concentrate his research on Protestant seminaries because they shared a host of commonalities in such matters as governance, financing, and student body demography, which were quite distinct from those of the Catholic schools. Thus, when it became so immediately obvious how valuable Dr. Fletcher's work was for Protestant seminary leaders, it seemed important to attempt to put together a companion study for Catholic seminaries. Knowing of our desire to launch such a study, a Jesuit friend of mine introduced me to Sr. Katarina Schuth, OSF, early in 1984, and what a wonderful colleague she has been.

Sr. Schuth has been a member of the Sisters of St. Francis of Rochester, Minnesota since 1960. She received her Ph.D. in Cultural Geography from Syracuse University in 1973 and was subsequently, professor, associate academic dean, and dean of admissions at the College of St. Theresa in Winona, Minnesota. In 1982, she left St. Theresa's to become first a student and then an administrator at the Weston School of Theology, the Jesuit Seminary in Cambridge, Massachusetts.

Since March 1984, Sr. Schuth has also been the director of the Lilly-funded study on *The Futures of Catholic Seminaries.* In that capacity, she has visited virtually every U.S. Catholic theologate and has conducted field interviews with more than four hundred seminary professors, administrators, and students. It could easily be said that she has gathered more factual data and information on the current seminary enterprise in America than any other single scholar.

It is now time for the American Church to learn from her vast and comprehensive understanding of the contemporary seminary. She has led a number of discussions of her work-in-progress at various professional seminary gatherings over the past several years, and last summer, she made a major presentation of her material to the Assembly of Seminary Rectors and Ordinaries. Last fall, the Endowment awarded a three-year grant that will enable Sr. Schuth and her research team to conduct approximately twenty-five dissemination seminars for church leaders, both here and abroad.

We are honored that one of her first public presentations of her research is taking place here at this FADICA conference. Each time I am with her I learn more, and so it is with great anticipation that I join you in welcoming Sr. Katarina Schuth.

SR. SCHUTH: It is always a pleasure to talk about seminaries, something about which I knew very little three or four years ago. Now I count among my friends and colleagues the four hundred people that have been interviewed as part of my research. I have found great vitality and health in the seminaries. As Archbishop Murphy mentioned, seminary educators are extremely dedicated to what they are doing, and they are doing a very fine job.

So it is with pleasure that I present some of the material that I have, and it is with appreciation for being invited to speak to this group, which is so important to the endeavors of the Catholic seminaries. The goal of my presentation is to report on four major aspects of the Lilly Endowment-funded research on *The Futures of Catholic Seminaries.*

First, I will speak about the mission and management of seminaries, including some comments on finances and governance.

Second, I will talk about the students, administrators, and faculty in seminaries.

Third, I will discuss the programs of seminaries: spiritual and personal formation, academic formation, and pastoral formation.

And, fourth, I will look at the future goals and future directions that seminaries seem to be taking in light of the needs of the Church today.

In the past twenty years, many positive developments and accomplishments have happened: excellent programs have developed; the personnel is of the highest quality; and the needs of the Church are being met in very significant ways. I will address all those things, but I will also mention some challenges and opportunities for the future, because not everything is settled in the Church today as far as seminaries are concerned. I will talk about vocations, enrollment problems, some of the staffing needs, some of the difficulties in meeting the needs of the Church, and the whole area of planning.

I would like to begin with a little bit of history (based on unpublished research by Joseph M. White). It is always good to put ourselves in context and to know that we have come a very long way. In 1563, the Council of Trent first decreed that there should be seminary education. It is difficult to imagine that the Church survived for almost sixteen centuries without seminaries. However, the response of people in those days to the directives of the Church wasn't quite as rapid as it is today. Not until the seventeenth century were there many seminaries at all, and then they were usually associated with cathedrals—many in France.

The first seminary in the United States was established almost two hundred years ago in 1791. It was St. Mary's in Baltimore, run by five Sulpician Fathers, with only four students enrolled. They had problems in those early days too. By 1799, there were still five faculty members, but only one student. The situation improved though, and by 1843, some twenty-two seminaries were open, with two hundred and seventy-seven students—thirteen per school. However, that wasn't the end of problems. Many of those seminaries closed, and the reasons sound like something that might be said today: a lack of local youth who were attracted to priesthood; an uneven supply of immigrant seminarians; a lack of clerical personnel to staff them; and a lack of regular funding for their operation.

So those middle years—that first half-century after the founding of the first seminary—must have been very difficult ones. And this continued until toward the end of the nineteenth century when the Third Plenary Council of Baltimore was held. At that time, a serious effort to renew the seminaries of this country began.

John Talbot Smith wrote a book called *Our American Seminaries*, and in it he said: "An ideal American diocesan priest should be an educated gentleman fitted for public life, physically sound, acquainted and in sympathy with his environment,"—isn't that what we would like today?— "and imbued with the true missionary spirit." This clerical model was a reaction against an older ideal of the priest as "narrowly schooled, whose mind was exclusively on the supernatural, and whose aestheticism and unexercised body rendered him sickly and useless, and whose European background caused him to disdain American values and to lack the flexibility for the very demands of ministry in America." So if we have a few problems with our seminarians not adapting to parish life today, imagine how difficult it was to provide transition in those years.

In the early twentieth century, the whole issue of modernism dominated, and there were some real setbacks for seminaries. At that time, seminarians were forbidden to read periodicals, and some directives contained these remarkable words: "it is important to control enthusiasm for learning." Serious discussion of theological issues just didn't happen, and scholarship was greatly inhibited.

In the 1930s, some professional organizations began to be formed, such as biblical societies, and these groups brought people together and helped renew interest in scholarship. This pattern continued into the 1950s, when considerable reform took place. Around that time the National Catholic Educational Association was established and it became an important horizontal contact among seminaries. It was a way they could exchange ideas and learn from each other.

In the early 1960s, seminary enrollment reached its peak. In 1961, counting all seminaries—high school, college, and theologate—there were more than forty-two thousand students in over four hundred seminaries. At that time, seminarians in the theologate numbered over eight thousand. In 1988, we are dealing with just over fifty theologates and just under four thousand seminarians in them, with an additional three thousand other students.

There have been enormous changes since Vatican II, including a dramatic series of relocations and reorganization of houses of study, schools of theology, and seminaries sponsored by both religious orders and dioceses.

You will notice that, at times, I use the word *seminaries*, and at other times, I use the word *theologates*. Theologates are the institutions that provide professional education for ministry, generally, the last four years of training for priesthood; seminaries could also be at the high school or college levels. I am speaking only about the theologate level, and that is pretty much what Archbishop Murphy was referring to as well.

In 1986–1987, fifty-four theologates were identified as members of the NCEA Seminary Division (see Appendix I). These schools are divided into three basic categories, with a few that don't fit into any category.

The majority of the theologates—thirty in all—are what we call "Free-Standing Seminaries"; that is, those schools that have all aspects of the formation program: personal, spiritual, academic, and pastoral formation. Even among these thirty theologates, you see many different categories, and their missions are also quite different—some are for diocesan seminarians, some are for religious order seminarians, and some include lay students. This fact points to an issue that Archbishop Murphy raised about the emergence of lay people in seminary education. In the early 1960s, as you will see in the figures regarding the number of students (see Appendix II), virtually no lay students were enrolled in theology schools. Now, counting both full-time and part-time students, well over three thousand lay students are studying with the four thousand seminarians. Many of the schools, at least three-fourths of them, have a mixed student body.

The second group consists of theologates that usually are related to universities and is called the "Supplemental Model." These are schools where the academic component is provided in a university—there are ten of those. In these settings, the personal and spiritual formation is taken care of in a house of formation.

The "Collaborative Schools" have a variety of expressions; two of the very large ones are the *Union Model* schools: the Catholic Theological Union in Chicago and Washington Theological Union in Silver Spring, Maryland. Those are the two largest schools in terms of total number of students, each with over three hundred. By contrast, many of the other schools, about half of them, have fewer than fifty seminarians in each. So, you can see how precarious the state of those very small schools is. Another kind of collaborative school is called the *Federation Model*, where several institutions work together. An unusual combination of three small schools in Washington who relate to each other is termed a *Mixed Model*.

In the "Other" category, there are the Melkite, Byzantine, and two Cistercian religious seminaries as well.

The data that I have relates to the schools that are listed in Appendix I. When we come to the question and answer session, if you have any questions about the differentiation of those schools, I would be happy to answer them at that time.

I would like to move now into a short discussion of the seminary models and the changes that have taken place.

Some seminary educators hold that it is best for seminarians to be separated from others while they are being educated for the priesthood. And they have some very good reasons for this. The belief is that it is preferable during those years to focus exclusively on the *meaning* of priesthood, per se, and that it is not simply the *teaching* of a theology of ministry that is involved—which a lay minister might do—but rather it's more focused on priestly ministry. In addition, they feel it is also better for the seminarians to be separated in a more reflective environment.

Those who have chosen to change the model and have made the seminary—the theologates—open to a variety of students feel that it is in the best interest of the seminarians, and of the Church, that they be educated in a setting that more closely represents the population in general. The Church today requires that priests address issues from various perspectives, including that of the laity. And that means that if, in the process of education, they can interact and sometimes even argue with their lay counterparts in the classroom, it can really help them later on when they become priests.

So, you do have these two very different viewpoints. As you might expect, the first report from the papal visitations tends to favor the first model: seminarians only, with limited lay contact. One of the consequences of that stance is that seminaries have not felt—with a few exceptions—free really to engage in dialoging about what it means to educate lay ministers today. That is a task that is before the Church: to look at how that is going to be done. As a matter of fact, many seminaries would find it difficult to stay open if they depended only on the enrollment of seminarians. So, if these seminaries are going to continue to enroll lay students, there needs to be discussion among those who are educating lay people, to find ways to do it more effectively. Both ordained and other professional ministers need to learn how to work in a collaborative setting where the authority of the Church is respected. A number of seminaries are working toward achieving that model, but I would say that we don't have a good model at this point. I see this as a major task.

In one questionnaire that I did, fifty-three out of fifty-four rectors and presidents responded when I asked them to list three changes that have taken place in their seminaries in the last twenty years. I didn't say list positive ones or negative ones, but all except five or six were *positive* changes. They said that they made the changes because of the needs of the Church and because of the theology of the Second Vatican Council. When asked what the impact of change has been, they said that the quality of priesthood education has improved, and the quality of theological education has improved. So the impact, from their point of view, is an extremely positive one: these have been good changes for seminaries, and they are better than they were twenty years ago.

Continuing on the question of mission and management, I will say a few words about governance and finances. A recent part of my research has been to look at who serves on the boards of trustees of our seminaries. Not counting the university boards, there are forty-one separate boards of trustees that serve at the first level of authority. An additional twenty-two advisory boards also exist, so that makes a total of sixty-three boards that serve our seminaries not associated with universities. On those boards, there are eight hundred and twenty people. Two-thirds of them are clerics; one-third are lay people.

I have met many of those board members and the quality of person that serves is outstanding. Today, however, they really need to have a better sense of what is is they should be doing: getting more involved with decision making and, often, with fund raising. In their view, the Church needs to learn how to share power and control and authority. This is a real challenge. It is very difficult to give up authority because it is a great risk to do that.

One of the reasons that boards have expanded, certainly, is for financing. Seminaries have always been the "favored children," in a sense, of the Church and sometimes of the bishops who are funding them. But these days, as resources decline, it is becoming more difficult to finance seminaries. About thirty seminaries are sponsored by religious orders, and these religious communities of men pour literally millions of dollars into these enterprises. There is very little recognition of their contribution. It is not at all uncommon for a group of men religious to be donating three hundred to five hundred thousand dollars to seminary education so that the tuition can be kept low.

Over forty percent of those who teach in seminaries are men religious. That pool of men became available when many of their own schools closed in the early and mid-1960s and the two large Unions were formed. Thirty or forty orders gave up small seminaries to join the two Unions. As a consequence, many men who were teaching in those seminaries then became available to other seminaries. Many of them are interspersed throughout dioceses and throughout the seminary system.

That pool will soon be diminished, and since it will need to be replenished by lay people who need regular salaries—not big salaries but at least somewhat commensurate salaries—the costs escalate and finances become more and more difficult.

Of particular concern is the inability of the Catholic schools to give scholarships comparable to those given by institutions such as Yale and Harvard. Weston School of Theology is located in Cambridge, very close to Harvard Divinity School which has many Catholic lay students, in part because they can give more scholarships than Catholic schools. This kind of enrollment pattern is happening with many non-Catholic divinity schools and is an area that needs some attention. Bishops are concerned about this problem. More and more, our future Catholic leaders are being trained in the Protestant divinity schools because that is where they find funding. And until the finances of our schools can be assured with endowments or scholarship funds, the probability of attracting many more Catholic students is reduced.

It is not as if the seminaries are standing by doing nothing. Development programs are being established in many of the schools. Over half of them now have well-organized programs, in large part, started through a Lilly project.

Let us now move to the personnel of seminaries. The number of administrators in seminaries has increased considerably along with the complexity of the programs. This has happened because, with the introduction of lay students, it was necessary to establish separate personal and spiritual formation programs for them; to expand the number of classes; and to have a variety of student services available. Moreover, the formation program—the spiritual and personal formation—and pastoral programs for seminarians also have become more specialized and, therefore, more people are needed to staff them. We have moved from a simple system of perhaps two or three administrators—the rector-president and the dean— to ten or twelve administrators, with particular growth in the areas of student services and finance and development.

For rectors and presidents, the turnover is very high. This is a concern for the future, because with that much turnover, the continuity and the sense of history is lost. It is also more difficult to ensure that there will be good planning. Those who serve in these higher offices of the seminaries have roles that now involve considerable external work and responsibilities: fund raising, recruiting, maintaining the reputation of the school, belonging to national organizations and professional organizations. Coping with those responsibilities, plus trying to keep the school going, has meant that there is tremendous pressure, and they simply don't stay in office for long. The same kind of thing, for different reasons, is true of the position of dean.

In noting the structures and observing how seminaries have expanded, what is needed is an analysis and redesign of administration in light of the new complexity that is present in the seminaries today. The schools need to look critically at what they are doing and then plan in new and different ways for the needs that they have.

About nine hundred faculty members teach in the fifty seminaries. (See Appendix III.) About three-fourths are priests and about one-fourth are lay men and women, and women religious. This proportion is, of course, a shift from the years when virtually the entire staff was priests. The quality of those who serve in seminaries, I believe, is extremely high. Just over two-thirds have a doctoral degree, and about one-third have a master's degree.

Faculty, like administrators, tend to feel overworked and overextended. They are expected to fulfill a dual role that includes not only teaching but also responsibility for personal and spiritual formation. It is not enough for faculty simply to know their discipline, they have to be persons who can relate to students on a whole other level of spiritual development. If we are to have young men who are able to relate to people in parishes, a tremendous amount of personal effort is needed on the part of seminary faculty.

And so, as seminaries look toward the future—a future where the number of men religious and priests as teachers is declining, and where women are underutilized in various capacities—there will be real problems finding faculty unless some planning is done at this point.

The other part of the personnel at seminaries is the students. I have already mentioned some facts about the numbers and the different types of students. If there is any one area in which rectors and presidents would like to see improvement, I think it would be in the numbers of students available to them. Seminaries compete for the small pool of people who want to become either priests or lay ministers in the Church. Unless that number is increased, we will soon suffer from a lack of trained people to serve the Church, ordained or lay professional ministers.

Students are very interested in service to the Church. Their motivation is definitely to serve other people. There are concerns, however, on the part of vocation directors and those who recruit with regard to the quality of students who are being recruited. The way it was explained to me is that those who used to fall into the top ten percent academically are no longer entering seminaries. In other words, that upper cut is, for the most part, gone. The rest of the students are about the same academically, so there is not a significant drop in quality. However, with the upper group smaller than it ever has been, there is concern when we think about leadership, and when we think about future educators in the Church.

A very important question, then, is how do we encourage vocations? Also, how do we encourage those who might enter lay ministry? Fr. Gene Hemrick, who will be speaking later, has a great deal of data about students, and you might address some questions to him.

A third dimension I would like to talk about is the programs of seminaries. I mentioned that there are three aspects of the program: (1) spiritual and personal formation, (2) academic, and (3) pastoral formation.

Students consider spiritual and personal formation to be most central to their preparation for a future ministry as priests or as lay ministers in the Church. The programs have improved greatly over the last ten to fifteen years. We have learned so much in secular society about the kind of psychological impact that the society has on students: what kinds of changes need to take place in them; what kind of ministry they are entering; and, therefore, what kind of person he or she needs to be. This personal and spiritual formation is developing well, but the training of those who are conducting the programs is probably not as good as it could be. Only in the last few years has there been specialized training, and more will be needed in the future if we are to avoid potentially major problems.

The academic formation that is taking place has improved tremendously in the last two decades. About twenty years ago, Catholic theologates joined the Association of Theological Schools, and I think that has made a great deal of difference in the quality of academic education. Students, by and large, really enter into these programs—all important to their formation.

One persistent question: "Can faculty teach everything that needs to be taught in the few years that students have?" And the answer is: "It is very difficult." I think the schools do well in scripture, moral theology, and systematic theology. They are beginning to do more on pastoral preparation. But in areas such as how to work collaboratively with lay ministers, and particularly women, in parishes and how to deal with conflict—those areas are not routinely part of the curriculum. And yet, those are areas in which the young men will need some training.

Administration and management are other areas in which very little can be done, simply because of the limited time frame. But now, young men are becoming pastors at a much earlier age than in the past. If you go to Kansas, Minnesota, and Montana, just to name a few places, after one or two years, a young man is put in the position of being a pastor. That is a tremendous pressure for a young person with little experience. I don't think anyone in this room is twenty-seven or twenty-eight. But remember what it was like at that age; it was not easy to be in charge of anything. And the young men realize they don't have this kind of preparation. I think that has to have an impact on the vocational question as well.

The field education of pastoral formation is an area that has been given great emphasis since the Second Vatican Council. This is an aspect of training when the young people who are entering into ministry "practice," so to speak. They do an internship; they go into the parish and begin to work in many different ways. Some do it in a block of time—for three or four months; others spread it out through their whole time in the seminary. For example, there is the "teaching parish," where the person is involved in a parish for four years and really becomes part of it. The goals of those who are directing the field education—the supervised ministry—are to get more participation from parishioners, to help students see how parish structures are changing, and to have them become more aware of the collaborative model of ministry.

All of these formation programs relate, of course, to the needs of the Church today. And that's the last thing I would like to talk about. The needs of the Church are multiple and manifold, as we all know. The ethnic groups that were mentioned by Archbishop Murphy; the aging population; the young people—how can we relate to all of them? How can we develop the sociocultural perspective that is needed to understand the various situations from which people are coming? Many of them are not imbued with the faith in the ways that we were, as children. You know, we learned the catechism; we learned about our faith; we learned the doctrines of the Church in a much more systematic way. Now, young people have different approaches. When they come to seminaries, they often are unaware of some of the basic things that we assume they would know. Yet, in a few years, they will be out of the seminary, where they will be dealing with well-educated Catholics—Catholics who are much better educated than they were twenty or thirty years ago.

The whole immigrant population has changed in terms of ethnic groups. We must develop ways and means of helping the large number of Hispanic and Asian people who are in need of the services of the Church. This poses a challenge for the future.

Another change, which I think is a serious question for both seminaries and the Church at large, is the shift of the Catholic population to the South and the Southwest in the last fifteen to twenty years. When we look at the location of seminaries, they are primarily, in the Northeast or the Midwest. This unbalanced distribution of seminaries is in need of some shifting and adjusting.

In facing the future, something else that I think is quite essential is planning for seminaries. I went through all the catalogs of the fifty or so schools, and only five have directors of planning listed. Planning has not been done in seminaries to any great extent, but I think that it will be in the future. If planning does not take place, decisions are made without the necessary background and information. Planning is needed not only on a local institutional level but also on a national level, because without it, I think we will have poorer allocation of resources and lower quality schools.

Another thing to be considered for the future is an evaluation of the ministerial effectiveness of those who become priests. Such an evaluation might look at the differences in the various seminary models. Does it really matter in what kind of a school or seminary a student was educated? Does it matter that it was one in which there were only seminarians? Is it better if the seminary was a mixed model? We don't know the answers to these questions, but I think they would be the source of some good research.

To summarize, I would like to recap my four points: mission and management; personnel and students; programs; and future goals and directions. I think we are concerned with both survival and quality. It is not one or the other. It is really both.

Concerning mission and management, we have the issues of what kind of school is best; the emerging role of boards; clarifying finances and building endowments; and distributing the charges for seminary education more equally.

With regard to personnel and students, the issues include ongoing training for major administrators; design of administrative structures; training for second-level administrators; faculty development; student scholarship programs; ministry transition programs (continuing education for new ministers); and transitional programs (return to seminary for reflection periods).

Concerning programs, curriculum development is needed to address some of those issues from *A Shepherd's Care:* How to serve in parishes that are very different; collaborative ministry; matching the needs of the parishes with the kinds of services that can be rendered; dealing with conflict; and dealing with different groups of people.

And finally, with regard to future goals and directions, operational and strategic planning is central. In addition, meeting regional needs (e.g., the population shift and dealing with the variety of people being served) and measuring ministerial effectiveness in the context of the Church today are all important areas that need our attention.

My final comment is one of hope. In the course of the past three years in doing this research, I have been touched deeply by the quality of persons serving in this special task of preparing men for priesthood and others for church ministry. The dedication, skill, and goodness of their work makes me believe that all things are possible for a spirit-filled future. And your cooperation and participation in that, I think, is very important. We may all be surprised by the direction in which the Spirit leads us, but let us pray for each other, that we will be open to the Spirit.

PANEL DISCUSSION

MR. HOFHEINZ: Fr. Robert Sherry, who is the executive director of the NCCB Secretariat of the Committee on Priestly Formation, will moderate our panel. A priest for the Diocese of Rockford, Fr. Sherry has served in this role for five years.

To his left is Fr. Eugene Hemrick, also an Illinois native, who teaches at The Catholic University of America and is director of the USCC Office of Research. He is also the director of the ten-year *Lilly Studies on Current Students in Seminaries*.

Next, we have Fr. Vincent Cushing, OFM, a Franciscan of the Holy Name Province, who is the president of the largest seminary in America, the Washington Theological Union. Fr. Cushing is also the Dean of American Seminary Presidents.

Our next panelist is a Vincentian priest, Fr. David Nygren, CM, who is a psychologist by training. He teaches at Boston University and Weston School of Theology. Fr. Nygren has been Sr. Schuth's co-director in this study.

And last, but not least, is Fr. Charles Froehle, who is the rector of the Saint Paul School of Theology in Minneapolis-St. Paul.

At this time, I would like to turn the microphone over to our moderator, Fr. Sherry.

FR. SHERRY: I would like to congratulate the people who planned this conference. You have assembled a fantastic panel of experts here. The people who are serving on this panel are some of the finest researchers in the field today.

As a panel, we will debate some of the issues and problems of the seminary today. We will spend some time predicting what form the future of priestly formation might take. I will also ask the panelists to state their basic principles or beliefs about priestly formation. Lastly, we will give the audience an opportunity for questions and answers as well as for comments and insights.

I would like to start off with a more focused context. My thesis would be that presently, we are in a critical time. We are at the crossroads in priestly formation programs. We are doing remote preparation for the fourth edition of the *Program of Priestly Formation*, the book that guides our seminary programs. This year, we noticed another decrease in enrollment in our student population: two percent on the theologate level; twelve percent on the college level. It is a critical time because we are having great difficulty in finding a priestly faculty for our formation programs. It is a critical time because of the increasing number of minority Catholics in the United States, especially Hispanic and Asian. It is a critical time because we're actively debating the nature and definition of the priesthood. It is a critical time because we are actively debating the direction of models of priestly formation in the seminary.

Allow me for a moment to be a little dramatic. Panelists, let us pretend that this meeting is your last chance to say what needs to be done in this critical time. The question would be: How would you respond from your experience and your research? Let us begin in the order in which you were introduced.

FR. HEMRICK: I agree with Fr. Sherry's assessment. I work very closely with him, as well as with many of you here. I do feel that right now we are at a crossroads. In looking at the research over the last few years, it does confirm—at least in my own mind—that we are faced with many problems.

First of all, we have a much older group of men coming into the seminary. One-third of our seminarians are over the age of thirty-five. When you have older and younger men coming together in the seminary community, a seminary rector faces a number of the ramifications.

Let me give you an example. I was with a seminarian who was driving me back to the train station after a meeting in Newark, New Jersey, and he said "You know, we have quite a few older seminarians here in Newark."

And I said, "Oh, that is interesting."

Then he said, "They go home every week."

I said, "Well, most seminarians can go home now."

He said, "No, they go home because they have to go home; some are taking care of parents, and some have businesses that they haven't quite left."

That was the first time that I realized we really have two different types of seminarians, with the varying age groups. In the past, when a seminarian went into the seminary at eighteen years of age, he moved completely into the spiritual world of the priesthood and there he immersed himself. It was a new world, and, to some degree, he left the other world behind. Today, many of our older seminarians are in both worlds.

Another ramification of the mix of young and old is that our missionary outreach is not as great as it once was. When you have older men, they are less apt to go to the missions at forty or fifty years of age. They just don't have that zest that comes with youth.

We do have more Hispanic seminarians than before, and we need them because that is where many of us are focusing today. But they are not the only group. Let us not forget the Asians; we have many Koreans, Vietnamese, and Cambodians today who are looking to the priesthood. Nor must we ever forget the blacks, who were neglected by the Church when this country was just beginning. How do we bring all these groups in?

Another problem we face was found in our most recent study. A group of seminarians was asked, "When there are fewer priests, how are you yourself going to face priesthood?" Thirty-seven percent told us, "We are going to go it alone." The other group said, "We are going to work closely with the laity."

As we go through the numbers, it becomes obvious that we have a mixture of apples and oranges when it comes to today's seminarians versus what we had years ago. Half of our seminarians do not have formal religious education backgrounds, which puts many of our seminarian professors into the role of being remedial religion teachers. Some of our seminarians do not have the traditions that you and I take for granted.

And then—as Sr. Schuth's study shows—today, we have rectors who are turning over every four or five years. What does that say to long-range planning? What does that say to that community called a seminary? And what does that say to us today when we compare it with the past? Many of these seminary rectors are being put into roles similar to their secular counterparts: they must be fund raisers; they must go out and shake hands; they have to worry about numbers. It is almost like being a businessman who has to market his product. But what happens to the unique role of seminary rector? Is it too nostalgic to say that he should try to capture the life spirit of the seminary and be more immersed in its daily flow of events?

One of Sr. Schuth's findings that needs serious consideration is the question of mixed seminary population versus a totally separated male population. It is something that is not going to go away; that question has to be studied.

Another question that needs our attention: How do we keep the academic level of our professors high?

This all leads me to the conclusion that we need to have a person in the seminary who is in charge of planning and research. We need to have someone who is looking at ways of taking this mixture of people and welding them together; someone who is examining ways of upgrading the academic levels of a seminary; and someone who is looking at ways of putting the rector back into the role of being with his seminarians, rather than just being on the road all the time. This whole new role of planning and research is going to be very important in the future.

I don't think we have the answers to the future. We will always need somebody who is constantly tracking, reflecting, and then moving—operating in ways that best meet the specific problems. It is an ongoing endeavor.

FR. CUSHING: I approach the whole question from a specific perspective—that of working in a Union seminary. I believe the seminary exists for the Church, but I believe the Church exists for the world. And I always insist that the question be addressed within that large framework. Consequently, the educational issue about seminaries really is an attempt to answer the pastoral issues of: Where is the Church? What does it need? And with what will its schools be dealing?

Within that particular framework, then, I look to a couple of processes and approaches rather than, say, issues of content, or sometimes the political difficulties we face in the contemporary Church. I look to issues of quality: What is the best education that can be provided for these students, whether they are eighty—as was our oldest alumni—or whether they are twenty-three? What is the best education for them? And within that context, I look at the issue of the integrity of the educational processes: What is good research? Who is a good scholar? What is academic freedom in these United States? How do we relate to the larger Protestant and Christian experience in America? What do the empirical sciences have to say to us? Those are the seminary and education questions. And I refuse to be pushed off into a Catholic ghetto educationally and to deal with it in a rarefied world where the air gets very stale very quickly. I insist that we have to keep in the mainstream of what education is about, face the hard questions early, and refuse to have them politicized or ideologized by the far right or a far left, by a conservative, by a liberal. What I am interested in is quality in that educational process. If you can give me good students, and I can give you good faculty, then perhaps we will have decent ministry long after I am dead.

Now, I don't mean to oversimplify the process. That is a terribly difficult and complex process when you reduce it down. But I suggest that those ultimate values of Church and world; of pastoral concern that is truly faithful to the nature of the gospel; of a quality in education; integrity of processes; and quality selection are where the future of the American Catholic Church is in regard to the issue of ministry.

FR. NYGREN: I would like to state my issues and address my concerns in two areas, both of which are reflected in Fr. Gene Hemrick's and Dr. Dean Hoge's study. They found that there are two reasons why young men are interested in becoming priests: (1) they experience an inner calling; and (2) they respond to external callings by looking to priests who provide good examples, envisioning a happy life, and wanting an opportunity to serve.

Within that context, I would like to read some results of a recent study I did on leadership within the executive level of religious congregations. The survey of eight hundred men and women religious provincials indicated that neither males nor females find a high degree of optimism or expectation of support from the institution of the Church. More specific, fifty-five percent of the males and seventy-four percent of the females responded that the current atmosphere in the Church was suspicious rather than trusting. And thirty-seven percent of the males and sixty-three percent of the females found the current climate of the Church quite dissatisfying. Similarly, twenty-seven percent of the males and fifty-one percent of the females surveyed believed the institution of the Church to be static rather than dynamic and faith-filled. Both males (forty-seven percent) and females (seventy-one percent) reported a high degree of turbulence in the current life of the Church.

The purpose of my giving you these statistics is to set up the juxtaposition of what would attract a young person into ministry in the Church versus the lived experience of those who are attempting to lead the Church today.

Furthermore, within this same research project, fifty-three percent of male communities anticipate significant decreases in their own enrollment, if not absolute extinction as congregations within the Church. Only twenty percent of the men's congregations expect any sizable or even moderate increase in membership. These results suggest that the priest's example and the turbulence of the Church provide a milieu within which it is very hard to be optimistic about the future of ministry as it is currently experienced.

Nevertheless, we know, from our evangelical counterparts in other churches, that the inner calling is very strong among those pursuing ministry. We see that in women in our Church. We see that in young people in our Church. But for some reason, we do not observe the same strength of inner calling among many men preparing for the priesthood. Within the group of people that we do attract to seminaries, some are highly competent; others appear to be high-risk candidates, in that they exhibit behavior and attitudes considered socially inappropriate for public ministers of the gospel. And contrary to the initial expectations for older candidates, some second-career individuals manifest instability in their personal and professional commitments; to this extent, they are considered high-risk candidates.

My question, then, is twofold: What model of seminary would be conducive to the development of the inner call that individuals feel? And second, How can we provide better examples of what priesthood really is?

In our experience of the fifty seminaries in our study, we contrasted two different types, if you will, and we saw most institutions on a continuum between what I call an *identification model* and an *integration model* of seminary education. This was derived by looking at what I observed in the programs as well as in the student bodies that we interviewed.

First, in the identification model of seminary education, the programs are basically derived from one role example or model: What is a priest? How does the priesthood mirror the ministry of Jesus? And so on. They start with a fundamental assumption and then derive programmatic dimensions and techniques from that assumption. That is acknowledging that the role of the priest in the world is a profession, that it is a leadership role, that it has ecclesial dimensions to it, and that it is quite specialized within professions.

The identification model of formation has two governing principles: There is expected compliance to a certain set of behavioral norms that govern what it is to be a priest. Second, there is typically—and this is increasingly less the case—a lack of routine interaction with the larger ecclesial community to which these people are expected to minister. Consequently, you see among some, a role rigidity: they identify with the role of the priest, sometimes at the expense of their own personal integrity.

They too quickly identify with what the priest can do and what the priest appears to be as the role model. That can have the effect of splitting the public and the private person. They quickly want to become a priest, to assume the trappings and the responsibilities of the priesthood, and they are not necessarily integrated enough to assume those responsibilities.

On the other end of the spectrum is what we call, for lack of a better term, the "integration model" of seminary education, wherein we find the role standards moderated by a process of critical self-reflection, an emphasis on pastoral formation, and quite often, an emphasis on external training programs such as CPE. Many of the programs being developed by seminaries recognize the fact that the students, be they lay or cleric, need to have their behavior and the roles that they have adopted, tested in a cross-situational validation process. By that, I mean they need to have a milieu broader than seminary in which to test their ability to be ministers—to live out that inner calling rather than simply the role of the priest.

So, again, we are back to the two reasons why young men become priests: one is that they experience an inner calling; the other is that they live up to a priest's example. What I am suggesting is that the models have got to mesh the two issues. They have to emphasize and continue to highlight the inner-faith dynamic in a developmental fashion through the programs that are being developed. In my view, this has to be a cross situational validation experience; it needs to be in a situation that is comparable to what the seminarians will face upon ordination. And finally, they should be educated with laity.

There are various shapes that these programs can take, but, as Mark Twain once said, "Nothing is so shallow as a value untested by temptation." We have some hybrid programs that look great on paper, but they have never been tested by the real world ecclesiology—the people, the grass-roots faith that is emerging. And yet, we sometimes continue to reinforce a program that is quite stylized and revolves around what Zirzola (1978) referred to as "hieratic prudence," as opposed to "evangelical *humanitas*," as the governing principle of priestly identity. I think the laity of the Church have picked up the "evangelical *humanitas*" and are running with it. However, we have yet, as bishops, priest, and laity combined, come to enough dialogue to understand what "evangelical *humanitas*" looks like or to consider its impact on priestly life and identity. And when all else fails, we revert to the force of office over *humanitas*.

FR. FROEHLE: I am always very grateful for the kind of research information that's available to us who are rectors of seminaries and people in seminary work—the kind of work that Sr. Schuth and Fr. Nygren have done, and the kind of work that Fr. Hemrick has done. My task is to try to translate all that research into a seminary setting and see what can happen with it.

There are a couple of things I would like to touch on from the comments that have been made this afternoon, beginning with Fr. Sherry's assertion that "this is a crisis time."

I think I could agree with that, but I wonder if, as we look back twenty years, we should have recognized that it was a crisis time then. There were a hundred and ten seminaries twenty years ago; there are fifty-four today. We didn't know then what we expected. I don't know if twenty years from now there will be twenty-five seminaries against the fifty-four of today. But having said that, it seems to me that the crisis is a crisis of the Church. And we have to make that understood. It's not a crisis simply within the seminaries. We deal with that, and we see the results of the diminishing numbers of candidates. We see the tension between how you educate them and what you are looking for. But unless and until the whole body of the Church accepts this as its responsibility, I don't think we are going to make too much progress.

Sr. Schuth talked about the growing role of boards of trustees within the lives of seminaries. And she pointed out that one-third of the membership of boards is lay people. That is healthy because it does involve the broader Church in the dialogue and in facing the issues and trying to deal with them. I think that aspect should increase and grow because seminaries need that kind of input.

But we also need that input in the educational process itself. I want to talk about that for a moment, in terms of questions that have been raised about faculty: Where are we going to find priests to teach? How are we going to prepare students to meet the kinds of needs that Archbishop Murphy cited from *A Shepherd's Care*? I think there, too, we have to depend upon the broad experience and involvement of the Church in order to deal with those issues.

It is said over and over again that priests must be on seminary faculties, and I would agree with that. But the question is: In what roles? And to what extent? An answer that is given almost immediately is that they are needed because they have to model priesthood. I am not sure, however, that a good academician priest is the best model for a student who is going to be a parish priest. Certainly, that person can model a prayerful life, an interest in theology—and that is very important—celibate living, and values of community. But in terms of what it means to be a parish priest—and that is mostly the kind of training I am involved with—they tend not to have the same kinds of insights as the parish priests would have, because they don't work with it on a day-to-day basis.

So, how are you going to find that modeling? I think we need it and are discovering it in the area of field education. It seems to me that the contact with parish priests, people who are working in parishes, and the involvement of those people in seminary programs, which has grown over the last decade, is critically important to the right kind of modeling of a parish ministry for the student of today. There they see a priest not just talking about what it would be like in the parish—as I can do in a seminary setting—but they will see a priest doing it, and they will have that person next to them saying, "this is how it is done." Or not saying anything to them, just letting them observe it and working with them. That is a modeling of priesthood that is, I think, often overlooked in the discussion. It takes place in supervised ministry—the working of students in parishes—and has to be recovered because it is closer to the experience that these people will have, than is the modeling that takes place in seminaries.

Again, I think it is critically important to have priests on the faculty and in good numbers, because there is another kind of modeling that needs to be done, a certain bonding that needs to be done. But there is an extraordinary number of fine lay people who make very good seminary faculty, who have great dedication and, again, who involve the life of a larger Church into this process. They can help us in making seminaries today what they need to be. They will help humanize, in ways that I cannot as a priest. The lay men and women provide a variety that can be very helpful.

We seem to think, when we look at the statistics of the declining number of priesthood candidates, that maybe we don't have as generous a group of people responding to the call to serve the Church today as we once

did. However, some of the other statistics that Sr. Schuth cited—that there
are as many lay men and women seeking theological education for ministry
as there are priesthood candidates—would suggest that there is a large
body of interested people. We need somehow to encourage them, help
them, and learn from them as we go along.

FR. SHERRY: I am sure that the members of the panel must have some
ideas that came to each of them as the others were speaking. Let us take
a few minutes for an interaction of reflections among the panelists before
we open it up for general discussion.

FR. CUSHING: One of the points that Dr. Dean Hoge makes in his written
research touches on a point that Fr. Froehle made about the issue of crisis.
Dr. Hoge says: "In another configuration of reality, there is no crisis. We
have exactly the same amount of altruistic people willing to serve the
Church." The difficulty is that we are dealing with a configuration of
ministry that insists it must always be a celibate ministry rather than the
religious being celibates, and that it must be a lifelong commitment.

He also says: "All of the research says the candidates are not there. But
if you deal with the issue of altruism and dedication, and people willing
to serve in ministry as lay ministers, we find an extraordinary amount of
generosity amongst our young and older people."

Our difficulty is—and, to a great extent, it's understandable—that we
are a Church that is growing arthritic, and we need to overcome that
arthritis somehow. There is a world out there that is looking at us and
waiting for us to join some of those great human questions and address
them. I suggest that seminaries are some of the better places to educate
people for that, as opposed to, say, the pickup courses that are offered in
some of our Catholic colleges and universities. Seminaries and schools of
theology that have been dealing with those particular issues for many
years have a certain sense of the pastoral mission of the Church that is
invaluable in terms of creating the right atmosphere for people to learn
ministry.

So, I think a future is there, but the problem is our own vision.

FR. FROEHLE: I would like to elaborate on that. There is that tension
between a separate education for priesthood candidates and a mixed model
of education. We have talked about that as one of the issues of theological

education today. In that discussion, however, we have to make sure that as the lay person is prepared for ministry—and that's happening, and I think it should happen—the whole Church must take responsibility, not just an academic institution, as generous as it might be.

I think Fr. Cushing's point is very good. The seminaries have experience with these things, and also they are the appointed group, mandated by the Church to prepare candidates for the priesthood. But who is the Church asking to prepare lay people for their ministry? That's my question. The Church has to take responsibility for that. The seminaries are there, and many of them are willing to take on that responsibility even though it's not easy to deal with the mixed model of education. One of the key elements in all this, however, is that the Church must say: We see the need; we want to offer the education; we want to offer the possibilities. And if the seminaries don't do it, how will the Church take responsibility for that education? Or will they leave it to academic institutions and maybe not be satisfied with the results? I think the Church has to care about it.

FR. HEMRICK: I would like to address the idea of this being a critical moment for seminaries. There have always been critical times in the world, and they can serve as a lesson for us.

Recently, I was reading the book *Mask of Command* by John Keenan. It is a story about four generals: Alexander the Great; Wellinton; Ulysses Grant; and an anti-heroic general, Adolph Hitler. It is very interesting. As war progressed, it has thrown different armies into disarray—just as today's seminary system might be looked upon as being in disarray. When Alexander was fighting, in which times they fought at swords' length, the leader was always up in front. But as the ballistics got better, the leader went to the rear of the battle line. As the way of fighting changed, so did the approach on how to fight.

One of the most interesting developments in warfare was the Corps of Engineers, which was first established at West Point to meet the changes in war strategies. In Roman days, they utilized engineers to build ramparts around cities. But it was not until the 1840s that a Corps of Engineers was developed to meet the new demands of modern military strategy.

I wonder, as I look at the disarray in our seminaries, if we can't interpret this as a new war—it's definitely a cause we are fighting for—and maybe, what we need today are new introductions like the Corps of Engineers.

We are at the crossroads, to use Fr. Sherry's word. Some might call it the Phoenix, rising out of our own ashes. It is a tremendous opportunity for anyone with an engineering mentality to build new systems to meet future demands. What we need now are people who can think in terms of new systems and bring a fresh mentality to confront the challenges we face.

And, if we are "arthritic" as Fr. Cushing so well stated, what better way to fight that arthritis than to take it as a challenge and, again, to think in terms of new systems by attacking and building new types of ramparts. We are not dead; it is just a matter of putting our imagination to work.

FR. NYGREN: One other thought I had in response to that is the issue of gender within the Church. I think it is crucial to the identity of the priests and the future of the Church in this country, and significant research needs to be done to determine how gender impacts the experience of ministry.

Recently, I have been working with the National Pastoral Life Center, giving workshops in three different cities around the country. In two of those cities, I have found priests to be highly emotional over this issue of being called to work with women in a responsible, collaborative way. They don't know what that means; they don't know how to build a team. My research as a psychologist is mostly around the issue of gender. When I attempt to work with these priests and these lay women and religious women, it is precisely the dynamics that occur within three- and four-member teams that indicate how gender influences that interaction. It is very difficult for a young person to learn how to relate to the opposite sex in a single-sex environment. When they get into ministry and find themselves in conflict, how do they negotiate with the women? Since the priests are the leaders, what happens to the women who are cast off because they don't have the same power to reward or to fire a person? That is a critical issue for a lot of diocesan priests.

The other crunch they experience is being caught between the hierarchical demands of their office and this expectation of an undefined philosophy of collaboration, a matrix model of ministry that is so ambiguous and so dangerous as to be lethal. It makes the life stress for priests very difficult to endure.

I have found that when men and women come together in a supervised setting, they *can* negotiate, and they can learn from each other—as the research suggests—that men and women are equally competent and can do the same thing equally well; they just do it differently. The way men bond with each other, the way women bond with each other, and the way men and women bond together, varies. Just understanding the dynamics of feminine psychology or masculine psychology, in terms of the way people move toward cooperation, is a critical component of education for ministry. However, I don't know of anywhere that that occurs in seminary education.

FR. SHERRY: Three of the four panel members were ordained in 1963; the other was ordained in 1977. You may or may not notice some differences in perspective. Some of us, when we think about seminaries, may have thought of a separate institution, confined, refined and distant. Yet today, we are hearing some issues that are somewhat foreign to that vision of seminary.

Fr. Froehle mentioned that twenty years ago there was twice the number of seminaries as there are today, and perhaps, twenty years from now there might be half the present number. Should we let the next twenty years happen as the last twenty have, or is there a design that we should help to implement? Do we have a sense of what priestly formation is? Do we have a sense of how that relates to lay formation and collaboration? Can we dare enough to make that happen? Or should we let the Spirit lead? I guess I am looking down the corridor of time and asking your wisdom.

FR. CUSHING: It all depends on if the future is in our hands. And that is part of the issue that has to be addressed on an ongoing negotiated basis. And where that future goes will depend on whether we are mature enough to take our history into our own hands. It seems to me that the jury is out on that question.

FR. FROEHLE: Some time back—1979 perhaps it was—the CARA/Lilly Study on Seminary Finances was done. There was a good bit of information provided from most seminaries in the country. One of the comments was— and it is still applicable today—if we don't formulate directional plans for the next twenty-five years, then, almost inevitably, it will be finances that make the decision for us. About that same time, I was in conversation with a seminary faculty person who had just described a new program that the seminary had initiated. It was an exciting program, he said. Unfortunately, the seminary closed down that year because of finances.

We need to look very closely at funding seminaries in this country. But how do we finance a seminary? We have had a long tradition of local care: dioceses that sponsor their own seminaries; religious communities that sponsor their own. There is very little national—or even regional—financial planning for priestly education today. I think we need that planning, along with planning about issues, if we are going to allow the best ideas to come to the fore. In a sense, because of our long tradition of autonomy from diocese to diocese, it is very difficult to have cooperative dialogues. But unless we talk about it, it will never happen.

FR. HEMRICK: After being in an office of research for twelve years, I often wonder whether this thing called *planning* is priestly. Believe me, there are those who believe that this is not a priestly role, that it really doesn't matter, and priests should just go out and minister from day to day. And after you work with numbers for a while, you do get the feeling that maybe there's something to that. You can use the argument that the Holy Spirit is eventually at the core of everything, and yet as you sit and look at planning for the future and the question of whether or not we should be planning, I think it is an obligation.

Romano Guardini has a fabulous book called *The End of the Modern World,* in which he says that if we are to avoid a nuclear holocaust, leadership has to practice certain virtues: earnestness, gravity, and asceticism. *Earnestness* he defines as getting the facts. It is one thing to build bomb shelters; it is another thing to discover who is building the bombs and why. *Gravity* is sorting things out in the midst of chaos. It is that ability of a leader, even though things look chaotic and in dissaray, to stay in there and to sort it out. And, of course, *asceticism* is the moral fortitude it takes to accomplish this.

The roots of Guardini's thesis can be traced back to St. Thomas Aquinas' two virtues: wisdom and counsel. St. Thomas puts it so well when he says, "the virtue of wisdom is getting at the ultimate causes in life." And if we are baptized and we believe in the Holy Spirit and the seven gifts of the Holy Spirit, one of those gifts is the gift of *wisdom.* For *counsel,* he uses the words "a research of mentality." It is the whole idea of sorting things out by taking counsel all the time.

So, when anyone asks if we should be planning for the future, I think the answer in that we are obliged to do so because of our baptism. And that is why I am staying in research as a priest.

FR. SHERRY: At this time, I would like to invite questions from the audience. Mr. Robinson?

MR. ROBINSON: With regard to the mixed model question, is there a value in distinguishing between the three areas of formation? For example, you have a mix in the academic area, but a separation in the spiritual formation and personal formation.

SR. SCHUTH: Yes, in fact, that is very much the way it is. Those places that now have a mix of students, I would say, universally have separate programs of formation for those who are preparing for priesthood and for those who are preparing for lay ministry. Sacramental ministry is so central to the role of priests, and it is becoming even more central, I think, as the number of priests declines. The kind of preparation that is needed for that—both spiritually and personally—is a little different from what lay people need to prepare for a variety of ministries. There are some aspects of that formation that can be done together, but by and large, the programs are separate. Pastoral formation, too, has different goals, depending on the type of ministry that the person will enter.

DR. BUTLER: Sr. Schuth, both you and Fr. Froehle talked about finances. My question is, if you were to poll your seminary rectors on the general topic of finances, what specific areas would they identify?

SR. SCHUTH: I am sure different persons would have different responses.

First, it would depend on the type of institution. There are those that have large physical facilities and, of course, upkeep and maintenance is a big issue. Another concern is space utilization. For example, there are seminaries that were built for three and four hundred people that now have a hundred or fewer. So that is one kind of need.

Then, there is the increasing number of lay people on faculties and in administration. Compensating them equitably is another area of concern that many would have.

Third—and I think this would be true for virtually all of those seminaries that have a mixed student body—would be scholarship money, particularly for lay students. Though it can also be a real problem for priesthood students from some dioceses. Those are just three areas that come to mind.

FR. HEMRICK: I just want to add one thing from our statistics. When we asked the seminarians in our study whether or not they needed financial help or whether they were in financial difficulty, I believe it was twenty-four percent that said they were in immediate financial difficulty. They were in a seminary situation, but they were in debt.

FR. CUSHING: With the brain drain that is going on in seminaries, in terms of the better professors gravitating toward universities, the issue of faculty development becomes terribly important. We need to keep some of our premier scholars in seminary situations where they can deal with that. But many of our seminaries don't have good sabbatical funding or programs, especially our diocesan seminaries. That is a big issue.

FR. FROEHLE: I would like to elaborate on something that Fr. Hemrick said. More and more of our diocesan priesthood candidates who complete their seminary program end up with very high debts, due to escalating tuition fees and room and board charges. Many seminarians are asked to repay their debts—or at least a portion—after they are ordained. In some cases, a student may end up with a thirty thousand dollar debt upon ordination. That is a morale issue.

In the last three or four years, I have also seen an increasing anxiety on the part of students over simply having enough money for day-to-day living expenses. So, direct aid for students is a greater need now than it was five years ago.

DR. LANGAN: I would like to ask Sr. Schuth, reflecting back on your vast research, were there any particular kinds of seminaries that were more successful than others at attracting an unusual number of vocations and actually being able to retain those interested people and see them through to ordination?

SR. SCHUTH: Yes. I think there are two types of places that would fall into that category.

Actually, the overall retention rate is quite high. It's a bit difficult to measure because some people take four years and some five, so we don't have statistics on a person-to-person basis. But, in general, retention is quite good.

In terms of attracting, however, there is one kind of seminary that has attracted a lot of students lately—those that have only male students. But that is partly an ecclesiastical issue. Bishops, in many instances, are choosing those seminaries for their students because of the Vatican's inclination to say that is the better way to do it, in spite of what the American experience seems to be. The other kind of seminary would be the larger schools that have a much larger faculty and are known for the quality of their education. Those schools have a mix of religious priesthood candidates with lay students.

So, it is really the two extreme opposite types of seminaries that are attracting students. That seems to reconfirm the tension that we have been discussing.

FR. CENKNER: I would like to see a follow-up on the retention question: How many people are retained in ministry five years after ordination? Ten years after ordination? I would like to see some research done on seminaries in terms of how long their priests have stayed in active ministry.

SR. SCHUTH: I think that is an extremely good research topic for the future. Some individual seminaries have tracked their graduates, but a national research study would be fascinating.

PARTICIPANT: No mention was made in the presentation about the growth of clerical vocations in Latin American countries and in Africa. Are there any parallels there of lessons that are worthy of observing in their religious education?

SR. SCHUTH: I haven't been to too many other countries, but I did spend a good deal of time in India, and I know that situation well; which would be comparable to Africa in terms of numbers of vocations.

A variety of factors is involved: One is certainly the kind of cultural values and attitudes that are present in our culture. Another dimension, which is in a sense negative to those other countries, is than many of those who are attracted to a seminary may be attracted for reasons other than vocation or God's calling. In poor countries, it is an opportunity to get an education and an opportunity to be well-fed. I lived in a convent in India for about six months, and they had well over two hundred young women who wanted to enter. The same was true of young men wanting to enter the seminary that was close by. They knew they could be educated and then move on and out if they decided not to stay with the order. Certainly, the value of self-sacrifice is often greater in those kinds of settings, and we could well imitate that.

FR. HEMRICK: I once asked the Archbishop of Chile why they had such a large number of vocations. He said that Catholicism was the other end of Communism, and there was such a contrast between the two, that many young men saw Catholicism as the way of combating Communism. It was very attractive to them because it gave them an ideology.

FR. NYGREN: That goes back to the point that I made earlier about the clarity and identity of the role of the American priest. Unless you have a clear perception of what you are to become, why would you want to become it? Or, if there is not a clarity of vision around the functions that you will be asked to assume, what are you signing on for? I think that the role diffusion in the American priesthood is a critical issue and needs some consolidation. If we can clarify the identity and the function of the priest in ministry, I think it will be a step in the right direction toward a higher retention rate. Then formation programs that assist individuals to integrate the actual role, and not merely the functions, will be much easier to develop.

MR. HOFHEINZ: We are all grateful to the panel members for their keen insights.

WHAT IS A PRIEST?

Speaker

Rev. M. Edmund Hussey

Pastor
Saint Paul Church

Panel

Rev. Charles Kavanagh

Executive Director, Seminary Department
National Catholic Educational Association

Rev. Thomas F. Gleeson, SJ

President
Jesuit School of Theology at Berkeley

Rev. John E. Rybolt, CM

Rector
Saint Thomas Theological Seminary of Denver

Rev. Gerald L. Brown, SS

Provincial
The Sulpician Fathers

Rev. Joseph Cunningham

Rector
Saint Vincent De Paul Regional Seminary

MR. HOFHEINZ: Fr. M. Edmund Hussey is a priest of the Archdiocese of Cincinnati and currently serves as pastor of St. Paul Church in Yellow Springs, Ohio. Ordained in 1958, he has a master's degree in both classical languages and English from Xavier University and earned his Ph.D. in historical theology from Fordham University. Until 1983, he was a professor at Mount St. Mary's Seminary of the West in Cincinnati and served that school as its assistant dean. Fr. Hussey has taught theology and religious studies at such institutions as Xavier University, Edgecliff College, and the University of Dayton. He has also served as director of the John XXIII Institute for Eastern Christian Studies. In 1963, he received a Fulbright Scholarship for study in classical archaeology at the American Academy in Rome.

Fr. Hussey brings a distinctive perspective to this conference. Though he has impressive scholarly credentials, which I outlined ever-so-briefly a moment ago, he currently serves as a local parish pastor in his home archdiocese. His role as a scholar-pastor qualifies him in a most special way to discuss with us his chosen topic: "What Is a Priest?"

FR. HUSSEY: Thank you very much. Although I have spent many years in seminary work, it is primarily as a parish priest that I speak to you today.

Our discussion yesterday certainly showed that seminaries cannot be addressed in any kind of splendid isolation. Questions about the Church and, indeed, about the world in which we live are an integral part of discussions about our seminaries.

But perhaps most immediate and most pressing is the question about the priesthood itself. My talk today has been quite simply labeled "What Is a Priest?" It is important at the outset to remind you that there is no simple answer to that question. As Karl Rahner frequently pointed out, the priesthood has been and continues to be a very complex phenomenon in the Church. What I intend today is a personal theological reflection on the priesthood. I shall reflect on the theological tradition of the Church as I have studied it and as I have attempted to teach it, and also on the priestly ministry in the Church as I have experienced it.

I begin my reflections with Sr. Ann Simeon, who died this past summer. She had taught me when I was in the seventh grade. Our diocesan paper said that she was ninety-five years old when she died. She was an excellent teacher—one of the very best—and a very lovely person. She had an enormous influence on most of her students, myself included.

Sr. Ann Simeon was a great promoter of vocations to the priesthood, as were most nuns of that era. She knew exactly what the priesthood meant and was very clear about the identity of the priest. The priest was truly another Christ, an *Alter Christus* who spoke in the name of Christ. As Christ on earth, the priest said to infants: "I baptize you," and to sinners: "I absolve you." Above all, at Mass the priest stood in the person of Christ and said over the bread and the wine: "This is *my* body; this is the cup of *my* blood."

I remember Sister telling us that the priest could call God down from heaven to the altar, that only the priest could do this, that no one else in the world had the power to do this. Many of us naturally were quite impressed and thought seriously about the possibility of becoming priests.

But Sister Ann Simeon was a realist, not a starry-eyed visionary, and she told us plainly that there were also costs—great costs—if we were to enter the seminary. We had to be good students, willing to study for many years. We would have to live a very disciplined life. We should not expect to become wealthy. We would not even have a home of our own and would have to go wherever the bishop sent us. Above all, we would have to give up marriage and a family of our own.

Sister's vivid and dramatic presentation of the priesthood was, in fact, a very sound, reasonable, and orthodox one. It was based solidly on the Tridentine theology of the priesthood, which emphasized the priesthood as the principal ministry in the Church, and whose starting point was the sacramental powers that belong to the priest alone and set him apart from the laity. The principal sacramental power, of course, was the power to change the bread and wine into the body and blood of Christ. To quote a medieval Latin formula, the priest had the *potestas in Corpus Christi eucharisticum*, the power over the eucharistic body of Christ.

The Tridentine era of the Church died in October 1958, less than five months after my own ordination to the priesthood. On October 9 of that year, Eugenio Pacelli, known to the world as Pope Pius XII, died at Castel Gandolfo. And on October 29, Angelo Guiseppi Roncalli was elected Pope John XXIII in the Sistine Chapel. John XXIII called a council, which would take a new look and, as it turned out, a non-Tridentine look, at the Church and the world.

This new council, the Second Vatican Council, did not emphasize the priesthood as the principal ordained ministry in the Church. The council documents clearly state that the priest participates in the ministry of the bishop, that the priest takes the place of the bishop in the parish and the priest depends on the bishop in the exercise of his ministry. The priest is now imaged as a stand-in for the bishop. The *Alter Christus* has become an *Alter Episcopus.*

Incidentally—and this is a bit of digression at this point—the new perspective on the priest as an *Alter Episcopus* is an important one. It inevitably makes dramatically new demands on the relationship between the bishop and the priest. In the Tridentine Church, when the priest was imaged as an *Alter Christus,* the relationship between the priest and the bishop was not nearly as crucial as it is today. Even an erratic and unreasonable bishop—and there were one or two of those—could generally be avoided and could even serve as a source of much amusement at clerical gatherings. After all, an *Alter Christus,* one who is another Christ, could quite easily survive estrangement from a mere bishop. But an *Alter Episcopus* cannot.

As important as the Second Vatican Council's emphasis on the bishop was, its emphasis on the whole Church, on the people as the Church, was even more important. Instead of beginning the discussion of the Church with the hierarchy, *Lumen Gentium* begins by emphasizing that the Church is fundamentally and basically the entire community of believers.

Although this emphasis sounds almost trite when so baldly stated, its implications were enormous. I shall mention only two of these implications, which have been of great importance to us priests.

First, if the Church is the entire community of believers, then the liturgy of the Church could no longer be a spectator sport at which the people watched someone else do something for them. The liturgy had to become once again the public work of all the people. In other words, no longer could I be a priest so that others did not have to be priests, but I had to be a priest so that others could be priests. I had to be a priest to enable the entire community to be a priestly people, a worshiping Church, a eucharistic community. No longer could I say Mass which others heard. No longer could I even celebrate Mass at which others assisted. Rather, the entire community must now celebrate a liturgy at which I would preside.

Second, if the Church is the entire community, then the work of the Church was not my responsibility as a priest, but was the responsibility of the people of God, of all of the baptized. No longer could I feel that I was entrusted with the mission of the Church in a special way and that the people had to support me in my work. I now had to realize that the mission of the Church is the responsibility of all who are baptized and that I have been ordained to assist them in that work.

I suppose, looking back at it, that is perhaps the most dramatic change in my ministry in thirty years. I was ordained to do the work of the Church, and you were supposed to support me in that. I hope that the young priests today have a better sense that you are all baptized to do the work of the Church, and they are ordained to support you in that. It's a very dramatic change in focus.

Therefore, the Second Vatican Council called us priests not to envision ourselves as a priestly caste endowed with special powers, but to see ourselves primarily as baptized Christians, and only then to see ourselves as those who have been ordained to serve the community of believers.

The earlier Council of Trent had summarized its teaching on the priesthood by characterizing it as the power of consecrating the true body and blood of Christ and of remitting or retaining sins. But the Second Vatican Council, in its *Decree on the Ministry and Life of Priests (Prebyterorum Ordinis)*, does not even mention the priestly power of consecrating the bread and wine. Instead, it begins with a discussion of the "Priesthood of the Faithful" and then speaks about all ministry in the Church as a means of enabling the Church to be the one body of Christ. *Prebyterorum Ordinis* affirms that the basic ministry in the Church belongs to the bishop, whose "ministerial role has been handed down to priests in a limited degree." This document teaches that the bishop fully possesses the priesthood of Christ (in the sacramental order), while the priest participates in that priesthood in a derived and dependent manner. The bishop is the sign of Christ to his flock, while the priest is a sign of the bishop.

Now, it is important to remember that *Prebyterorum Ordinis* is not one of the great documents of Vatican II. The major documents are the documents on the Church, on the liturgy, on the pastoral office of the bishops, on ecumenism, and on religious liberty. The *Decree on the Ministry and Life of Priests* is definitely among the minor ones. While it does say some fine things about the priesthood, it does not develop a contemporary theology of the priesthood. In fact, the Council Fathers took the priesthood for granted somewhat and did not feel that there was much need to discuss the matter at great length.

But, indirectly and unwittingly, the Council Fathers severely undermined the traditional role and significance of the priest in the Church. First, by insisting that the bishop is the primary minister in the Church and that the priest is the helper of the bishop, the Council demoted the priest from an *Alter Christus* to an *Alter Episcopus,* from another Christ to another bishop. Second, by emphasizing the priesthood of the laity and de-emphasizing the sacred power, which set the priest apart from the laity, the Council deprived the priest of his traditional identity and clear self-image.

In hindsight—and it is only in hindsight—the recent decline in the number of priests and the present straits to which we are reduced are the natural and, perhaps even inevitable, result of the documents of the Second Vatican Council. Now, I want to make it clear that the Second Vatican Council's emphases on the Church as the entire community, on the priesthood of all the baptized, and on the pastoral ministry of the bishop in the Church are all theologically sound and are all valuable corrections to an off-balance view that has prevailed for centuries. The fact that these emphases have created a great turmoil in our priestly ministry should in no way suggest that they are unhealthy and unsound developments. In fact, I am convinced that they are positive and enormously valuable steps forward. But the fact remains that they also raised important questions not only for priests but for the entire Church, questions that have not yet been answered sufficiently and satisfactorily.

There is no question that the priestly office and the priest's own understanding of his office are in a period of great transition. The Tridentine image still survives, of course, but it is no longer taken for granted and, indeed, is even challenged by many. Yet no new image has acquired clear enough outlines to take its place.

As I have mentioned before, Karl Rahner has insisted that the priestly office in the Church has been and continues to be an extremely complex reality. He cautions against any attempts to reduce this full reality to only one of its basic elements or characteristics. In fact, it is my impression that if there is a flaw in the Tridentine theology of the priesthood, it was that it reduced this very complex reality to one of its components and then saw that as the entire reality.

So, rather than make a futile attempt to present a neatly packaged theology of the priesthood, I would like merely to suggest two theological principles and five concrete characteristics of our priesthood as we actually live it. I will not, of course, develop them fully but only present them briefly.

My first theological principle concerns the relationship between the ordained priesthood and the priesthood of the faithful. In order to avoid a simplistic identification of the priesthood of the baptized and the priesthood of the ordained, church documents, ordination homilies, and theological articles frequently appeal to no. 10 of *Lumen Gentium*—the Second Vatican Council's document on the Church—to affirm that they differ from one another not only in degree but also in essence. But I want to point out to you that the sentence from *Lumen Gentium*, which is cited to support this essential difference, actually affirms a close connection between the two and merely presumes the essential difference. In the English translation of the council documents, edited by Walter M. Abbott, SJ, the sentence reads: "Though they,"—that is, the priesthood of the faithful and the priesthood of the ordained—"Though they differ from one another in essence and not only in degree, the common priesthood of the faithful and the ministerial or hierarchical priesthood are nonetheless interrelated."

Consequently, although we must not deny the difference between the two, the difference ought not to be overemphasized and used as the starting point for developing a theology of the priesthood. In fact, I believe that a search for the essential difference between the two as a *starting point* for understanding the ordained priesthood simply complicates the matter unnecessarily. I would suggest that the principal affirmation of that sentence in *Lumen Gentium*, the interrelatedness of the priesthood of the faithful and the hierarchical priesthood, might be a better starting point. It might then be easier to see that the ordained priesthood does not intrude between God and the priesthood common to all the faithful but, rather, enables the priesthood of the faithful to be fulfilled and effective.

My second theological principle concerns the relationship between the priest and the bishop. It is somewhat similar to my first principle. Just as an overemphasis on the essential difference between the priesthood of the faithful and the priesthood of the ordained creates unnecessary difficulties, so also I believe that an overstated attempt to *separate* the bishop and the priest will create other unnecessary difficulties.

In fact, throughout much of our history the exact relationship between the episcopacy and the priesthood has been a matter of some dispute. In the Tridentine era of the Church, the bishop was seen essentially as the priest, but with two additional sacramental powers: the power to ordain and the power to confirm. The post-Vatican II Church no longer tends to see the bishop in terms of the priest, rather it tends to see the priest in terms of the bishop. In the Tridentine Church the bishop was a "priest plus"; in the post-Vatican II Church, the priest is a "bishop minus." And that has been the difference in focus.

While leaving aside right now a complete development of this point, I do want to state the fairly generally accepted theological principle that the priesthood is not radically separate from the episcopacy. In fact, my next theological points will confirm that principle. For what I want to do now is list five concrete characteristics of our priesthood—those of us who are ordained priests—as we actually live it. These characteristics, which also have application to the episcopacy, are absolutely essential for understanding the priesthood.

First of all, by virtue of our ordination, we priests have a presidential role in the Church. We preside at the assemblies of the Church and we are the presidents of local churches in a very real sense, especially if we are pastors of parishes. The bishop, too, is the president of a local church— a local church that we call a *diocese* rather than a *parish*.

It is important to remember that in the early Church, there was no distinction between a parish and a diocese. Most cities of the ancient world were small towns by our standards. Thessalonica, Ephesus, and Corinth were most like our midwestern county seats than our large cities where we have bishops living. The Christians in those ancient cities belonged to one local church, to one ecclesical community, presided over by an *episcopos* (bishop) who was assisted by a council of *presbyteroi* (priests) and served by one or more deacons. The gradual development of parishes and the consequent distinction between parishes and dioceses is one of the most important and least studied developments in our structures.

At any rate, the local Church of the New Testament and the subapostolic era has no exact counterpart in today's Church. Legally, or canonically, the local church today is the diocese and only the bishop is empowered to ordain and, thus, provide for the continuing life of that local church. However, the parish is the real local church for most people today, for the parish is where they gather to celebrate the Eucharist, where they are baptized, where they are married, and where their funeral liturgies are celebrated. It is in the parish that they learn the tradition of Christianity, and it is from the parish that they derive spiritual nourishment for their lives and their work.

Second, by virtue of our ordination, we priests have an important sacramental and cultic role in the Church. In the past, there was a tendency to suggest that the full significance of the priesthood could be found in its cultic or sacramental function. The post-Vatican II Church has rightly insisted that the priesthood also includes very important prophetic, educational, social, and counseling tasks. However, the cultic function of the priest must not be belittled. The symbols, the rituals, the sacraments, and the liturgy of the Church are entrusted to us who are ordained priests, in a very special way. When I preside at the eucharistic liturgy, when I baptize, when I anoint the sick, when I bless marriages, and when I place ashes on the foreheads of the people at the beginning of Lent, on these and similar occasions, I exercise the priesthood most visibly and most profoundly.

Third, by reason of our ordination, we priests are ecclesial persons; we are authorized to act in the name of the Church. There are, of course, other ecclesial persons: bishops, deacons, religious sisters, professed brothers, and monks; all are ecclesial persons in various ways.

But within this group, our place is especially visible and recognizable, for we are the ones who are authorized and delegated by the Church, by the community of believers, to preside at liturgical gatherings and to administer ecclesial sacraments and to preach the ecclesial tradition. While some other persons are authorized to do some of these same things, except for the bishop, the priest has the most comprehensive and unqualified authorization and delegation to act in the name of the Church. And our exercise of this delegation is more familiar and frequent than the bishop's in the daily life of the Church.

Fourth, by virtue of our ordination, we priests are established in an especially close and publicly recognized relationship with other members of the Church. Whether I like it or not, because I am a priest, other members of the Church feel that I belong to them in a special way, that I have a commitment to be interested in them and to care for them. They feel that they have a claim on my time and my energy, and, if they are harshly rebuffed, they are very hurt and even feel betrayed.

Fifth and finally, by virtue of our ordination, we priests are symbolic centers of the Church, icons of the Church, a sort of embodiment of the faith and the values and the traditions of the Church. Now, certainly, the bishop is an even stronger symbolic center of the Church than the priest, and without doubt, the president of the College of Bishops—the Bishop of Rome—is a still stronger symbolic center and sacred icon of the Church.

The fact remains, however, that when people meet ordained priests, they do feel that they meet the Church and all that it stands for in a special way. This is a very precious and valuable asset for us, because it enables us to have far greater influence and effectiveness than we could ever have by ourselves. It also carries a far greater risk, as you know, for it will inevitably magnify the opprobrium and the stigma of our sins and our failures.

These five closely related characteristics of our actual lives as priests are certainly necessary elements in any comprehensive treatment of the priesthood. They are obviously only five aspects of a very complex reality, and I have not treated them in any depth. And so, I know that I have left far more unsaid, unexplored, and undeveloped than I have actually expressed. But I am confident that further reflection on these five points can help us better understand our priesthood in these changing times and exercise it more effectively.

I would like to take very briefly about two other items that quite powerfully affect our lives as priests, which I believe need to be addressed by the Church in a new and creative way.

First is the process of the selection of bishops. Although this is not particularly related to the conference topic, it is worth mentioning. I do not hold a brief for a particular method of choosing bishops and certainly not for the popular election of bishops. But I do believe, because of what I have said about the very close personal relationship between the priest and the bishop and between the bishop and the whole local church, that the local church should have an open, clear, and effective role in the selection of its bishops. I also strongly believe that American bishops should be chosen by the American Church in a well-defined manner and then confirmed by Rome, rather than appointed by Rome and then accepted by the American Church.

My suggestion is not prompted by any illusion that we will get better bishops in this way. In fact, my impression is that our bishops are generally above average in intelligence, in talents, and in dedication. My suggestion is prompted by a recognition of the increased importance today of the relationship between the bishop and the priests, and the bishops and the local church.

My second item, which is more closely related to the conference topic, is the process of the recruitment and education of priests. I believe that we need to search for other ways of enabling persons to become priests that are alternatives to the present system. I am not arguing for the abolishment of the present seminary system in which men make application to study for the priesthood and then, after some evaluation, are in the seminary, where they are given the theological, pastoral, and spiritual formation necessary for their future work. All of us who are priests here today were trained in that system, which has served the Church fairly well since the Council of Trent. And I believe that our seminaries, on the whole, still give very good training to those who study in them.

But the present method of recruiting and training priests is obviously no longer meeting our needs. The continuing decline in the number of priests in the United States is reaching an alarming level. On the other hand, we experience an increasing number of certified or commissioned lay pastoral ministers and ordained deacons, which certainly indicates that there is a large supply of generous and dedicated leaders willing to serve the community in a variety of ways.

It seems to me that we ought to explore the possibility of looking into the community for dedicated and talented Christians who are already recognized as effective leaders within the Church, and who might be called to ordination in ways that do not require going through the whole seminary system. Now, of course, that raises all kinds of concerns. Many of the proven leaders in our Church today are women and married men. Consequently, the questions of clerical celibacy and the ordination of women come to the fore again. I do, however, believe that premature and abrupt changes in these areas would cause more division and turmoil than improvement and advantage. On the other hand, it seems quite clear to me that both of these issues will continue to haunt us until they are confronted realistically.

I realize I have packed many undeveloped and controversial assertions into my presentation. But, in essence, I have suggested two theological principles that I think should govern the development of the contemporary theology of the priesthood: First, the ordained priesthood should be seen as the servant of the priesthood of the faithful. Second, there should not be a radical separation between the priesthood and the episcopacy.

I have further suggested five concrete characteristics of our priesthood as necessary ingredients of a theological reflection on the priesthood: First, the priest's presidential role. Second, and flowing from that perhaps, the priest's cultic role. Third, the priest's role as an ecclesial person. Fourth, the priest's very special relationship with other members of the Church. Fifth, the priest's role as a somewhat symbolic center or icon of the Church.

And, finally, I have suggested two additional processes, which I think need to be addressed in a creative way: the process of the selection of bishops, and the process of recruiting and training future priests.

I know that not everyone will find all of my reflections on these points sound or realistic, but I do hope that they are at least thought-provoking.

PANEL DISCUSSION

MR. HOFHEINZ: Thank you. Let me introduce the panel. Our moderator Fr. Charles Kavanagh, a priest of the Archdiocese of New York, is currently serving in his last months as executive director of the Seminary Department, National Catholic Educational Association.

To his left is Fr. Tom Gleeson, a Jesuit, who is the relatively new president of the Jesuit School of Theology School at Berkeley, one of two Jesuit theologates in the country.

Next, we have Fr. John Rybolt who is the president-rector of St. Thomas Seminary of Denver. He is a Vincentian priest, and his order is one of two major religious communities that have dedicated themselves to priestly formation.

Our next panelist is the Sulpician Provincial, Fr. Jerry Brown. His order is the other society that has dedicated itself to the training of priests. He is also a former seminary rector.

And finally, we have Fr. Joe Cunningham, a priest of the Brooklyn Diocese who now serves as the rector of the Seminary of Saint Vincent De Paul in Florida.

At this time, I would like to turn the microphone over to our moderator, Fr. Kavanagh.

FR. KAVANAGH: I thank Fr. Hussey for his paper. I would, however, like to put it in a slightly personal context. Since the completion of the Vatican Study and Rome's first response to us, a meeting was held at the Chicago Theological Union. Fr. Schrider, one of the theologians at CTU, gave a quasi-theological response to the letter that had come from Rome, making recommendations for our seminary community. It is ironic that his paper and Fr. Hussey's paper duplicate some of the same distinctions.

Certainly, there seems to be in Rome's initial response to us a clear statement about a personal theology of priesthood; by that, I mean the personal role of the priest as the *Alter Christus*. Fr. Schrider had commented that it seems that once again Rome's response to the seminaries reflected a bit of a return to the Tridentine concept of priests. No mention was made of the relationship to bishop, and no mention was made of the relationship of the priest as servant to the people of God.

The second major point that Fr. Schrider made was the same one that Fr. Hussey made: once again, the definition of priesthood seems to be highlighting the distinction of the priest from those others in ministry—much more so than emphasizing the relationships. And a definition that centers on *distinction* may not be as adequate as we would like it in terms of reflecting the question of priesthood and the lived experience of the Church today.

So, I resonated very favorably to the major thrust of Fr. Hussey's remarks because of that theological insight that was shared by Fr. Schrider earlier this year.

I think one of the most needed things to have in place during the next three or four years, as the American seminary community begins to prepare a new *Program for Priestly Formation*, is some serious reflection on the theology of priesthood. At a meeting of bishops and rectors of seminaries in July at Seton Hall, one of the four major issues raised was this question of the theology of priesthood. Ultimately, when you are talking about the priest and his role identity and the institutions that we have in place to serve them, the question that arises—especially as Fr. Nygren said, when you are inviting someone to enter into an ordained ministry—is not only "Who am I?" but "Why am I?" And that second question is critical: "Why am I?"

My reaction to some of the comments that came up in the five characteristics that Fr. Hussey cited is that I think some serious reflection is needed on whether or not those five characteristics of priesthood are by virtue of ordination. There is no doubt that they are in the lived experienced.

I would now like to open the discussion to the panel.

FR. GLEESON: In his paper, Fr. Hussey presents a number of issues and important characteristics that are associated with priesthood. In my response, however, I would like to address what I see as his major point, namely, Vatican II's view of priesthood, what he calls the *Alter Episcopus*. At the same time, I won't be looking at the shift away from the *Alter Christus*—another Christ—but, rather, at another implication, one that affects a significant percentage of the priests in the United States in a very important way. Fr. Hussey has at least *inferred* a challenge to the lived identity of the diocesan priest in that shift from *Alter Christus*. I would like to speak of a similar challenge to the lived reality of priesthood in religious life.

Fr. John O'Malley, SJ, writing on the same subject, characterizes *Prebyterorum Ordinis* (the document on the priesthood) as setting forth three essential aspects of priesthood: (1) that it is conceived according to a ministry that is exercised in a stable community of faith and practice; (2) that it is exercised most normatively in a parish structure; and (3) that it is exercised by priests who are in hierarchical union with the order of bishops.

Although the council document does allow for due qualification for regular clergy (i.e., religious order priests), the document clearly begins with the statement, "What is said here applies to all priests. . . ." So, evidently, the adaptations are seen as minor.

At the same time, the lived experience and tradition of religious order priests involve three quite different aspects essential to their priesthood. In the first place, priesthood for members of religious orders is primary ministry. In particular, ministry means apostolate or mission, which is being sent at the will of the superior to a wide variety of ministerial situations; at times, these are parishes, but they are also educational institutions, preaching, ecumenical work, retreats, social agencies, and so forth. Consequently, a second quite different aspect arises: ministry not simply to a stable faith community, but to whomever and wherever there is need—often direct evangelization while confronting atheism and unbelief. And finally, a third aspect is present, namely that the major religious orders have lived a long tradition of exemption from episcopal jurisdiction, again for the needs of the apostolate.

In short then, those are three very different characteristics that described the lived reality of fully thirty-five percent of the world's Roman Catholic priests at the time of the Second Vatican Council. In fairness to that council, it should be pointed out that the story of that tradition of religious order priesthood, though lived for almost a millennium, was not readily available to the Council Fathers. The history books on religious orders and religious order priests have been almost entirely histories of their respective spiritualities in community, not expositions of the meaning of their religious priesthood.

Put another way, Vatican II presents a notion of priesthood that combines the sacramentality and spirituality emphasis of the Council of Trent with a view of church *"office,"* which goes back to the patristic fathers. In so doing, it focuses on the bishop as pastor and the priest as his assistant. The tradition of religious orders, however, focuses on mission or apostolate. So, the former leads directly to the parish structure of ministry; the latter to a variety of corporate works and, ideally, to a mobility or readiness of response to new needs within the Church. In our day, the former is the ordinary mode of priesthood. The latter seems to have been the more ordinary mode in the early days of this country, but it is clearly the alternative today.

For a greater part of the long history of the Catholic Church, these two traditions have existed side by side and they do so today. Throughout that history, they have complemented each other and, thus, together have served the Church. Quite simply, they should continue to do so. Priests should continue to be trained in both traditions, and that will mean somewhat different ways of training those priests. If this does not continue, I would submit that the Church, in her mission to go forth and teach all nations, will be that much poorer.

FR. RYBOLT: Perhaps some of you have seen—and were as profoundly moved as I was—the film "The Last Emperor," by Bertolucci. In the film he chronicles the life of Pu Yi, the last Manchu emperor of China. In some ways, I identified with Pu Yi. He began life in one form of society, and then he went through revolution and was profoundly affected by that. And so have I been.

As Fr. Hussey has so cogently presented, the Church of our youth has undergone what clearly must be styled a revolution. This is especially true for priests and for those of us engaged in the exacting work of preparing others for priesthood. My purpose here is to elaborate on his paper by describing some of the changes—revolutionary changes—we have undergone. I do this with some hesitation because of the personal witness I am giving, but I do so in the same spirit exhibited in Fr. Frank McNulty's address to Pope John Paul II on his recent visit to the United States. His theme was: "If priests could open up their heart and tell of their priesthood." Priests, in his version, would speak of joy, consolation, responsibility, social concern, and the greatness of the people of God. Priests also experience sadness and worry over the credibility and future of their Church, over morale in the priesthood. But he spoke of hopes, shared charisms, collaboration with others—women included—and of our American need to question authority.

If we—priests—open our hearts to you, we can also speak of the actual exercise of priesthood. Many priests, in my opinion, are risking grave psychological danger as they increasingly say one thing in public, but believe something quite different in their hearts. Some of these things are simple embarrassments: "Father, put a special blessing on this medal." "Father, have you heard that the Blessed Mother had said such and such at a particular shrine and her statue was weeping?" "Father, how many Masses do I have to say or do I have to attend to get this indulgence?" "What if I break the chain?" "How much do I have to pay for this Mass?" These are embarrassments. But that's how things were when we were growing up.

Many priests are also confused and not just embarrassed in areas that are more transcendent: "What is the meaning of sin today?" "Is it really possible alternately to please and then to displease God?" "Can I, in good conscience, tell people they must, under pain of mortal sin, attend Mass on holy days of obligation on Saturday, and then come back on Sunday?" "Why is the Church so consistently interested in what happens in the bedrooms of its faithful?" And, paraphrasing Rodney Dangerfield, "Why don't I as a priest get no respect like I used to?"

We are still feeling the effects of the great Catholic revolution. Yet, speaking for my colleagues in the seminary business, we are, like Fr. McNulty, encouraged by many wonderful developments in spirituality, in collaborative ministry, in love for the poor, in historical and liturgical studies, in love for the Bible, and in intercultural experiences. To do our work effectively—a really noble work, full of promise for the Church— today, more than ever, we need the help, especially the financial help, of the people of God. But we rely also on their insights and their best thinking and the hopes that they have for their own lives and the lives of their families to help us understand how we should be exercising our priesthood.

FR. BROWN: I want to thank you for inviting us to be here. I really like the attitude of FADICA, which tries to open itself up to all the currents of the Church in order to make really intelligent decisions in terms of how its members can contribute. I am learning a tremendous amount from this whole group.

I am going to shift the focus to the seminary world because, in a way, I think it is between a rock and a hard place, in terms of how to handle all of these emerging issues.

When you look at all the seminarians coming to seminaries today, you find among them almost every type of theology, ecclesiology, and spirituality. And I think that people in seminaries would tend to agree with that. While there has been a shift from a pre-Vatican II ecclesiology and theology of priesthood to a more contemporary look, the pre-Vatican II Church is still very much with us in the United States, as well as all of the colorations of shifting up until the present time. Somehow, the seminary has to try to take a student from Point A and move him to Points B and C, toward priesthood. It is an extremely complex and difficult task. When you add to that the fact that every region of the country is different—

with different socioeconomic groups, ethnic mixes, and so forth—I think the seminary has a tremendously difficult challenge in trying to train an effective priest.

However, having said that, it is a challenge that we can approach with a good deal of enthusiasm, I feel, and with some sense of humor. And it is a problem that we don't have to bear alone; it needs the engagement of the entire Church, as was said so well by Fr. Froehle. Despite the challenge and the difficulty, we have to ask the question that Fr. Hussey just addressed: What is a priest?

Somehow, faculties have to come together in each institution. The Sulpicians have four seminaries in the country right now, and some of our institutions have done this better than others. But you have to come together as a faculty and make some decisions about where you see priesthood today in relationship to other ministries and in relationship in to the needs of the Church. That is easily said, but not very easily done, because on faculties you have tremendously mixed theologies of priesthood, different personal experiences, and different types of spiritualities. So, I think it would be a mistake for us to think it is an easy task.

It would also be a mistake for us to feel that we can even easily decide what a priest is today and what he might be for the next few years. We do not have a corner on the market of the future. Events determine an awful lot of what happens in the Church, and in all probability by the year 2000, we will be speaking a much different kind of language than we are today. I think you have to have a bit of humility and a good deal of courage in the seminary world and then eventually take a stand; keep in dialogue with the wider Church; and do the best you can to train adequate priests.

Fr. Hussey put his finger on some rather significant characteristics of the diocesan priesthood. I would also agree with Fr. Gleeson that a similar kind of picture needs to be created for the religious priest. I am involved mostly with diocesan priesthood, however, and from my perspective, I think one extremely important issue would be: If it is true that a priest is both ecclesial and presidential, how do you prepare a man to become those things? And what do you do with certain local churches where the president of the community is not the eucharistic sacramental celebrator of the community? If you are going to prepare a priest for a world that's becoming more and more unpeopled by priests, with larger numbers of lay ministers and sisters in ministry, with sisters and lay people becoming pastoral administrators of parishes, what happens to the identity of the priest in the midst of all that?

We are moving into a whole different experience of Church and leadership, and those of us in the seminary world are just barely beginning to catch up with it.

FR. CUNNINGHAM: I would like to comment on a few things in terms of the theology of priesthood.

First of all, one of the things that needs more emphasis is the gospel relationship of the priest—the preaching of the word and the gospel. There is a whole new emphasis on Scripture—the restoration of the books of the Scriptures to us as a Church—something that the priest would not necessarily see as important in the past. That emphasis includes the whole evangelization aspect of priesthood through the gospel and the question of homily versus the sermons of the past. But the word—the word of the priest, the word of the gospel—is an extremely important aspect of it.

The second thing that needs more emphasis is the presidential role— what it means to preside over a community. The whole question of presiding over a community comes from the fact of being related to the community. This idea of being the "walk-on" person and thinking you can talk to a community or preach the gospel or celebrate the liturgy within that community without having a relationship is absurd.

A third thing that we have to deal with is the "servant" aspect of the Church and the theology of the priest as servant in the community. The priest is the one who orders the ministries and needs to collaborate with those ministers to avoid being solely in that walk-on role, as itinerant sacramental confector of the Eucharist.

Our theology of the common priesthood and the priesthood of orders should not be a threatening theology. It is important to recognize that full status in the Church is not orders or commitment to religious vows; it is baptism, confirmation, and Eucharist. All of us are fully members of the Church, and we serve the Church in different ways. The priest is the full-time minister of the community, serving that community. That type of theology is there and has to be dealt with.

A fourth thing that needs to be addressed is the ecclesiology of the hierarchical relationship between the priest and the bishop. In that regard,

I am reminded especially of the Sacrament of Orders, which no longer talks about episcopal *consecration*, but rather an *ordination* to episcopacy. I think there are two types of things happening. First, role definition: Is it the "bishop"? the "priest plus"? or the "bishop minus"? And second, What is the Church saying about this?

The dangers that we have dealt with and the problems that we have had are important. But maybe they are *our* problems and not the problems of the future and the future priest. For instance, the challenge of other ministers is a problem of older priests. We have long memories, and priests do not seem to have the respect we thought we once had. But young people coming into the priesthood today—is this their problem, or are we imposing our frame of reference on them? Today, we are only one profession among many educated people; we are not the "answer persons" anymore. We can't deal with all of the necessary counseling by ourselves; we have to refer to experts in education or sociology. Whose problem is that? Is that a holdover from the past? Then, there is the ability to deal with a changing culture. This has been a problem, especially in large cities such as Miami, Los Angeles, and New York, where a priest who has been there many years is no longer accepted because the people's culture has changed. How does the minister deal with the new culture and recognize that maybe he is not the accepted person because he is not black or Hispanic or Haitian? How does he deal with that in ministry? We also have a problem of neo-clericalism crawling through seminaries and through the permanent diaconate—people who love to wear collars. At the same time, the present ministers move away from that, and want to minister in a theological way.

What about the seminaries today? What are the students' roles in some of these things? I think it is important to recognize how quickly generations pass. Things change. And people who are coming into seminaries today may not have all the problems that we had; they may not have the baggage that we had and may be ready, if they have had good ecclesial experiences, to deal with this area of collaborative ministries and, perhaps, with some of the problems that we are projecting on them.

FR. KAVANAGH: Thank you. I would now like to open the discussion to the floor. Does anyone have a question for Fr. Hussey or any of the panel?

FR. NYGREN: I would like to make a comment in relation to something

Fr. Gleeson said. When the Vatican II documents state that there are no longer three states of life within the Church, but rather two: the lay state and the clerical state, I think that reinforces what Fr. Gleeson talked about in terms of the dissolution of religious life both for women and for men. Consequently, women in particular have only one choice to make, that is to move in the direction of a lay state. Whereas men religious do still have the choice to identify as clerics, but they no longer have that third state, which was called the state of perfection. That issue really needs to be investigated, particularly in relation to monastic communities. If the priesthood and the Church are defined principally in terms of the parish context, the reason for a monastic community to exist becomes strained.

DR. BUTLER: When the Marshall Commission visited all the seminaries, to what extent was there an exercise that would have addressed itself to this very fundamental question of the nature of the priesthood, in relation to the philosophical bent of these institutions they were examining? Was that at all part of the picture?

FR. KAVANAGH: There was none. Very little dialogue took place. There was an assumption that we were coming to evaluate an institution, and it was a process much like a middle stage of a secular institutional process in terms of the evaluation of the program. We took the mission statement of the community and asked, What do you perceive as the purpose of this institution? What are you preparing a man for? You tell us, and then we will see whether or not your institutional program is meeting its objective.

FR. BROWN: One of our institutions was asked by the Visitation team, and then later by the final letter coming from Rome, to articulate in writing its vision of priesthood: "Precisely what kind of priest are you trying to train?" I think they sensed an implicit theology in the institution, but the faculty hadn't really carved out a particular vision for themselves. That was an extremely creative moment for that institution, when the faculty sat down and tackled a lot of these issues and, for better or for worse, made a choice in terms of what the institution stands for.

SEMINARIES AND THE LAITY
A LOOK AT WHO IS RESPONSIBLE FOR
MINISTERIAL FORMATION

Speaker

Mrs. Mary Pat Mulligan

Director, Family Life
Pontifical College Josephinum

Panel

Rev. Msgr. William L. Baumgaertner

Director
Association of Theological Schools

Sr. Mary Hennessey

Director, Ministerial Studies
School of Divinity, Harvard University

Rev. James J. Walsh

Rector
Mount Saint Mary's Seminary of the West

Rev. John E. Linnan, CSV

Associate Professor, Doctrinal Studies
Catholic Theological Union

Rev. John Strynkowski

Rector
Seminary of the Immaculate Conception

MR. HOFHEINZ: Our next presentation is both a symbol of how far the U.S. Church has come in the last decade as well as a reminder of how far we have yet to go. Let me illustrate by simply recalling some of the statistics that Sr. Schuth gave us.

Twenty years ago, any symposium on the American Catholic seminary would not have given a moment's thought to discussing our topic for this session: "Seminaries and the Laity." In 1968, every single one of the nearly eight thousand students in the U.S. Catholic seminaries—one hundred percent of them—were men preparing for the priesthood. And there was no reason to believe that this would ever change. Ten years later, in 1978, seminary enrollment had dropped to barely five thousand students, and very few of them—just nine percent—were not priesthood candidates. That is just ten years ago. Then came the explosion.

In the 1986-1987 academic year, seminary enrollment had climbed again and stood once more at just over six thousand, but what a significantly different mix they were. Only six out of ten were the traditional priesthood-candidate student. The others, fully forty percent of seminary enroll-ment—and I agree with Sr. Schuth that it's probably higher than that—were lay men and women. What a dramatic difference.

Our speaker knows more about this issue than I do, and I suspect she will be discussing it with us. But it is my feeling that most seminaries are only now beginning to wrestle realistically with the substantive ontolog-ical issues imbedded in this significant change in students. Seminary leaders are realizing that these increasingly large percentages of lay persons in their student mix mean more than just cosmetic changes have to take place in educational and formational programs. The whole issue is com-plicated, of course, by the obvious unease felt by many in Rome and elsewhere about this phenomenon.

Our speaker this morning personifies the very issue she will discuss. Mary Patricia Mulligan was one of the pioneer lay women in a seminary student body, having received her master's degree in theology at the Pon-tifical Josephinum Seminary exactly a decade ago, in 1978.

Since 1982, she has been an assistant professor of pastoral theology at that seminary, teaching courses in catechesis and family life ministry. In addition, she is director of the Theological Field Education Program and the Master of Divinity Program.

Mrs. Mulligan received her undergraduate degree from Carlow College in Pittsburgh and is currently enrolled in the Ph.D. program in systematic theology at Duquesne University. Married and the mother of three children, she is also involved in a number of diocesan projects including the training of catechists, teaching in the lay ministry training program, and consulting for the religious education department.

I join you in looking forward to her discussion on the role of the seminary in lay ministerial formation.

MRS. MULLIGAN: During the closing remarks of his homily for the synod in October 1987, Pope John Paul II said: "We bring the fruits of the work during the past month now to him who is the 'living stone,' to reaffirm that we too wish to be 'living stones' with which to go on building in history the edifice of the Church that is destined to outlast all time."

The purpose of my presentation is to take a look at the "living stones," to which the pope is referring and, perhaps, take a little peek into the cracks of the edifice. It will be important to note just how the "living stones" have been designed, determine the building process that has gone on so far, and then from those blueprints, project some future building ideas.

In preparation for this talk, I spent time reading about laity in general—laity formation, laity spirituality, all those things. The whole time, I kept relating what I was reading to my experiences since 1960. And I realize that I had grown up in a rather platonic background and had basically been formed in the whole world of ideas. My approach or my understanding of myself as a lay person, as well as my projections for the formation of people, now have a distinctly Aristotelian or an experiential slant. Given the series of events within the Church since 1960, and given the understandings that have arisen since that time, I am going to develop my arguments around the experience of the laity.

First, I will offer some autobiographical information on my own personal formation since I think, in many ways, it is reflective of lay formation. In the second part, I will comment on models being used for formation today. Part three will examine some of the contemporary challenges to lay formation. Then, in part four, I will propose some suggestions that sound feasible to me.

It is my impression that the experience of the laity in recent years has much to offer to the discussion of formation—how and where formation happens. As I look through my personal history, I can identify consciously with becoming a part of the "living stones" in 1960. At that time, my husband and I moved to a new city and registered in the local parish. Because I had a Catholic school background and was a certified teacher, I was asked to teach a high school religion class. Now, armed with those credentials and a knowledge of Thomas Aquinas, I was a complete failure at teaching senior high students. Those credentials weren't sound even then. However, my active volunteer life had begun. Between 1960 and 1972, I continued to be involved. While my children were young, teaching religion became my night out, my social world, my chance to meet people who shared similar values and family situations.

The experience of living in three different dioceses increased volunteer responsibility, and a heightened awareness of a potential mission led me to enroll at the Josephinum to work on a master's degree in theology. At the same time, I began working in a large parish in Columbus as the director of religious education. During that time of education and professional parish involvement, I sensed I needed something more, but I couldn't really identify what it was. So, I took more courses and I talked to more people. Gradually, my theological vocabulary improved, and I recognized I was really looking for some kind of spiritual guidance. Initially, I tried to satisfy that by taking a course on spiritual direction. But my volunteer and educational experience opened me to an articulation of the activity of God in my life, in the life of my family, and in the life of the people with whom I came in contact.

While I was working in the parish, I was very conscious of "living stones" being formed. The memory of that experience of working side-by-side with the parishioners has given me a grounding in ministry that I think I will always treasure. As I began in 1972, I saw my role then as a manager of a program heavily involved with logistics and organization. It wasn't very long before I became overwhelmed with the basic goodness of people and the sincere efforts of all the people with whom I was dealing. I witnessed people coming into a sense of who they were by exercising the fruits of their own baptisms, and I truly saw their lives changed in many ways.

In a recent article in *Praying* magazine, Clare Wagner talks about *enabling* and *empowerment*—I always say those are the only two jargonistic words I find useful. Clare Wagner compares *enabling* to the experience of the paralytic in the gospel when his friends brought him to Jesus: he was forgiven, healed, and thereby able to carry his own stretcher and walk away. *Empowerment* is what happened to the Samaritan woman. After her encounter with Jesus, she was able to talk about Jesus, to preach the good news.

I can truly relate to those descriptions as I think back, and I delight in recalling the names and faces of people whom I saw freed from their paralyses, whom I saw enabled and empowered to go out and preach the good news. The actors are varied; the scripts are as numerous as the individual; but the fact remains that enabling and empowering do happen as people develop an awareness of their identification as Christians.

The vocabulary of formation is used extensively in the literature describing the lay vocation. It is only my recent experience—that is, as a lay person working within the seminary environment—that I have come to a better realization of what really happened in terms of my own formation. The seminary experience has given me the vocabulary of formation and, therefore, the ability to describe myself within the parameters of the literature written about laity. The jargon of formation was not part of my volunteer activity nor was it part of my professional activity in the parish. I was so busy just muddling through the web of my existence, that the notion of a formal formation was not part of my critical consciousness.

Recently, a friend was talking, and said she felt she was learning to be a lay person "by default." She pointed out the *via negativa* categories: laity are non-ordained, non-clergy, for example. How do we know how to be vital lay persons actively engaged in the building of the body of Christ? I thought about her comment, and I wondered if maybe we aren't doing "formation-by-default" for the laity. In other words, What are the right stones? How are we turning over the stones to have truly "living stones"?

I don't think it's necessary here to elaborate on the laity's response to Vatican II's *Decree on the Apostolate of the Laity*. We are all aware of the increased involvements and responses of the people of God since that decree. People have examined their particular charisms, their particular life styles and vocations, and I think they have responded accordingly.

For our discussion today, I would like to look at the models that have been used as people have proceeded through the webs of their existence. Recall that we had to move from a hierarchial model, an ecclesiology from above, to an understanding of how to be the people of God. We began with our experience, that which we already knew, that which was readily available, therefore, we looked to the seminary model. Seminaries knew about formation. We looked to religious communities. Religious communities knew about formation; they also knew about the spiritual life. We looked to schools. Theology has long been a part of our educational tradition, and we knew that schools were capable of providing a basis for further reflection.

This brings me to part two then, a discussion of some models of formation available today. I look at those models I just mentioned—seminaries, religious communities, and schools of theology—and then I look at the 1980 statement by the National Conference of Catholic Bishops, *Called and Gifted: The American Catholic Laity*. I really have to question the validity of continuing to use the models of seminary and religious communities and theological schools as we discuss the formation of laity.

For me, *Called and Gifted* has been a very important document. It outlines a developmental model with which I am very comfortable, and it is also consistent with my experience of laity. It calls us to adulthood, a growing sense of who we are as members of the faith community living our daily struggles in whatever context that may be happening. Building upon that growing adulthood then, is a call to holiness. Paralleling the maturation is a deepening hunger for a greater participation in the spiritual life of the Church. Then the document sees a call to ministry, both in the world and in the community. All of these calls are exercised in whatever configuration that community may take, whether it is parish, family, the work place, and so on.

The development described in *Called and Gifted* is compatible with the thrust of the Vatican II decree as well as the propositions; most recently, the October 1987 Synod of Bishops.

I agree with Leonard Doohan as he talks about the mission of laity in *Laity's Mission in the Local Church: Setting a New Direction*. There is a greater sense of baptismal vocation today. Lay people, in many instances, are discerning their call and are living their lives based upon that commitment. More important, Doohan points to the "focusing on lay values," especially "where laity have expertise, such as family life, social justice, politics, war and peace." Studying the kinds of participation and commitment that are currently being exercised by the laity, Doohan says, "a new kind of lay person is emerging, neither fanatical nor extreme, but healthily committed and willing to struggle."

Within that context describing the profile of laity today, we still need to look to the documents and much of the other contemporary literature that keeps emphasizing the formation of the laity. Proposition 40 of the recent synod cites the formation needs: to have a more lively awareness of baptism and confirmation and participation in the Eucharist; to pay closer attention to the operation of the Spirit of God; to direct actions in the various fields of daily life according to the charity of Christ.

I have to ask the question, How will this be done? Again, I think we need to look at the experience. What is happening, and how are laity being formed? People are taking classes at seminaries. They are looking for a theological foundation both from seminaries and from schools of theology. They are also joining various ministry formation groups within the diocesan structure; these would include training sessions for youth ministers, family life ministers, and lay ministers, for example. Is this, however, the formation really being called for by the documents?

Within the seminary environment, I think laity are capable of receiving a good theological background. They are not, however, participating in a formation process that is tailored to their needs. According to Cardinal Baum's letter on theologates, seminaries should be specializing in priestly formation. Therefore, laity attending seminaries rightly can expect to receive a theological education, but their formation is to be happening elsewhere. I personally don't feel that the seminary can do both priestly formation and laity formation well. To try to do so only muddies the waters more. The distinctness of both clergy and laity becomes increasingly confused.

Generally, in the academic institutions, I would see a similar situation. Schools of theology will again give a strong theological foundation, but the formation will be dependent on the background, experience, and maturation of the individual seeking the education. The indicators of the formative value of courses probably are reflected in responses on exams, but I question the availability of follow-up and the intentionality of the formative process.

Presently, the specialized ministry groupings are trying more and more to include a formation/spiritual development component into their training programs. While I have seen some very strong efforts in this area—

and some very good efforts—I really suspect that a clergy formation model is oftentimes still at the heart of the program design.

Therefore, I see some problems as we talk about the formation of laity today, and it's these problems or challenges that I will address in this third part of my presentation. I would venture to say that is "formation-by-default." There are four major difficulties specifically involving formation that I would like to highlight.

First of all, at the present time, I see the growth and formation of the individual dependent upon the past experience of that individual. For some people, the seminary can become a fertile ground for developing spirituality because they have a readiness for the theological dimension. They also have the maturity to seek and integrate the theological education with their life experience. For people who have not had a rich formative background, the theological world of ideas may tend to keep them in the area of concepts, and those concepts are never going to provide the answers to their problems. Therefore, I feel that within the existing educational structures, be it seminary or school of theology, formation is going to be inconsistent and very subjective. I do not feel that formation can be presumed with a transcript or a degree being the criteria.

The second problem is a situation that confronts women studying in the seminaries or schools of theology. For many women, this experience heightens, sometimes even introduces, an awareness of exclusivity within ministry. Therefore, the theological setting, which is to be formative for the lay mission, may actually be the source of resentment for many women. In those instances, barriers are raised and integration of the spiritual development is hindered. Whether it is conscious or not, I think one of the reasons that Catholic women sometimes choose Protestant schools is because they feel they can receive a theological education that has a pastoral dimension in an environment that accepts women in ministry.

A third problem that needs further consideration is the expression of spirituality. The literature keeps talking about spiritual development, lay spirituality. Within Catholic tradition, we have extremely rich resources and examples of ways to live the spiritual life. The problem I see is that many times the spirituality that is presented as the ideal, is an ascetic or monastic spirituality. That is not necessarily the spirituality that best fits a busy, community-minded lay person. We need to adapt the formation of laity to acceptance of a variety of ways to live the spiritual life. Some people may choose to stay in the desert with John; others may choose to meet the multiple personalities that encountered Jesus. There has to be an accommodation, I think, for the "Marthas," the "Marys," and every other combination therein. I think we have the potential to resolve this problem, but until we develop and diffuse a spirituality from the experience of the laity, we are going to have a "spirituality-by-default" as well.

The fourth problem or concern that I have, means taking a long, hard look at the "living stones" with which we have been trying to build within recent history. I feel we are continuing to use the same models, and if we're not using them for the right reasons, then I propose that the life will be extracted from those "living stones." The extant foundation of the edifice is strong, but I don't think we can continue to duplicate the seminary and religious community models of formation if we are truly interested in the formation of laity for the twenty-first century.

So, those are some of the major concerns that I see, which are relevant to our discussion. Now, I will make some suggestions. These are suggestions, and perhaps some dreams, with potential results.

My first recommendation has to do with seminaries. At the beginning of the school year, I always meet the entering seminarians and ask them why they want to be priests. At that point in their formation, most of them talk about doing good things for people. As they elaborate, I find myself realizing that their expectations are not articulating anything that I, as a lay person, don't include as a vital part of my mission. I cite this example to try to illustrate why I support seminaries as a specific place for priestly formation. My hope is that within four years of formation, those now-entering seminarians will have an expanded notion of their charism as ordained priests and will emerge as the much-needed charismatic leaders in the Church.

However, I also have some seminary-related recommendations that will affect the formation of laity indirectly. The presence of lay people in classes with seminarians, which I strongly support, is a positive influence from which seminarians receive much benefit. There is *seminarian* formation going on, not necessarily lay formation. The heterogeneous grouping permits a wider base for theological discussion. Also, I feel that lay members of the faculty working with the clergy model collaborative ministry in a way that it cannot be taught in the classroom. Regarding the seminary curriculum offerings, I recommend courses in training that specify and highlight the role and mission of the laity, the formation and spirituality of the laity. This means really working from a laity-formation model rather than clergy looking at laity through a clergy-lens.

As an aside, I was wondering about the possibility of offering a course on comparative spiritualities, clergy spirituality/lay spirituality, a team-taught course with priest and lay person, for instance, doing the presentations. I think an honest approach to both of those would be something fresh that we have not necessarily seen in the seminary. There is much that can be done within the seminary that is both true to Cardinal Baum's recommendations and to the factors that will enhance the formation of laity.

My second recommendation revolves around a creative use of theological expertise. The reality is that there is a limited number of people who are trained as theologians and who are available to teach theology. Many of the experts are in seminaries and in schools of theology. Within any given diocese, there are some other individuals who are also capable. But how thin can we spread these people before the expertise becomes mediocrity? Therefore, I would like to see greater collaboration and more creative uses of the expertise that does exist in any given area. This means a blending of resources within various ministries and more flexibility of scheduling for seminaries and schools of theology. For instance, a diocesan lay ministry training program, a family life ministry training program, and the seminary could all share a scripture course. Seminarians may have to attend this one course at night, but one professor would be providing qualitative theological input for a variety of peoples. The formation would still be the responsibility of the individual sponsoring parties.

A third recommendation is that theological reflection groups be tailored specifically for the laity. According to Leonard Doohan: "Many laity who never think explicitly of theology still theologize insofar as a theology underlies their commitment and vision. There is probably more theologizing in the Church today than at any other time in its history."

My experience has taught me that laity do theologize. They do need places and situations wherein they can freely articulate their ideas about their experiences, where they can delight and rejoice in the experience of God in their lives, in the lives of their families, in the lives of the people with whom they work, and in the lives of the people they happen to meet. Spiritual direction is not the answer for everyone. Therefore, I am talking about many kinds of opportunities such as support groups, spiritual movements, spiritual companions, prayer communities, just to cite a few examples. Renewal programs in parishes have provided the beginnings of much theological reflection, but I suggest that there is much more to be done.

This leads me to my final recommendation. At this point in our history, I think it is crucial that our basic communities and our parishes realize that they are the vital "living stones" in this enduring Church. Pope John Paul II has been strongly affirming and encouraging families. Some work has been done, but I am afraid we have only scratched the surface. The Bishops' Committee on Marriage and Family Life has just prepared a book entitled *A Family Perspective in Church and Society* (USCC Office of Publishing and Promotion Services). This approach has much that is appealing, but it involves a mind-set that may require a reorientation for clergy as well as for laity.

In 1983, I was present for the conference at Notre Dame that was sponsored by the NCCB Committee on the Laity entitled "Work and Faith in Society: Catholic Perspectives." The participants were all leaders in their respective fields. As a group, their professional credentials were extremely impressive. The vivid memory I have from that conference is the plea I heard over and over again from those people concerning life in the parish. Generally, the parish was not providing the nourishment they needed. That memory is such a gnawing one for me. It tells me that the formation of laity must be treated with an urgency that is grounded in the basic communities of the lives of the laity.

There are implications once this kind of an approach is taken. The work to be done in parishes is going to require ongoing commitment and funding from the diocese that is addressing vital issues on the local level. These recommendations imply a new kind of training for both the clergy and for the professional individuals working in the Church. It means working with a sense of mission that laity bring rather than superimposing a mission on the laity. It may also mean recognizing credentials that are grounded in spiritual maturity and commitment—authentic holiness, holy "living stones"—rather than in academic degrees.

In her book *Laity Stirring the Church: Prophetic Questions*, Dolores Leckey says, "Something is stirring in Christian churches." The very fact that we can have this discussion indicates that we are looking at the activity, specifically the activity of the laity. I propose that we add some force to this "stirring" so that the laity are not "formed by default." By taking a positive approach to the formation of laity, grounded in the experience of laity, we can enable the Catholic to integrate the baptismal vocation to the extent that the mission called for by Vatican II will be articulated and exercised in a conscious way. My dream is that this "formed" Christian will be a vital force of the family and of the parish, with the potential to reach out to broader areas. In other words, I see the categories discussed in *Called and Gifted*—the call to adulthood, the call to holiness, the call to ministry and community—becoming the accepted norm rather than the exception to the norm.

From this pool of laity who have experienced a positive formation, I also propose that a more integrated Christian will be the profile of individuals presenting themselves as candidates for seminary training and future priesthood. People will be ministering for reasons grounded in gospel values. They will not be motivated because of a shortage of priests. Instead, there will be an urgency to be a vibrant "living stone" inserted into the foundation of this Church, this vibrant Church which, as Pope John Paul II says, "is destined to outlast all time."

PANEL DISCUSSION

MR. HOFHEINZ: Thank you. At this time, let me introduce our panel. The moderator is Msgr. William Baumgaertner who is currently the associate director of the Association of Theological Schools, the professional and accrediting association for seminaries—Catholic and Protestant—across the country. Prior to that, he was the director of the NCEA Division on Seminaries, and prior to that was the president-rector of St. Paul's Seminary in Minneapolis.

To his left is Sr. Mary Hennessey, a Religious of the Cenacle of Boston. She is the director of ministerial studies at Harvard Divinity School, and past director of the Boston Theological Institute, the consortium of Protestant and Catholic seminaries in Boston.

Next, we have Fr. Jim Walsh, a priest of the Archdiocese of Cincinnati and current president-rector at the Athenaeum of Ohio, Mount St. Mary's Seminary of the West.

Our next panelist is Fr. John Linnan, a Viatorian Father, who just recently completed his tenure as president of the Catholic Theological Union in Chicago. He remains a professor at that institution.

Finally, we have Fr. John Strynkowski, the rector of the Seminary of the Immaculate Conception on Long Island.

Msgr. Baumgaertner?

MSGR. BAUMGAERTNER: I will offer a few comments and then pass the microphone on to the members of the panel.

In going through the backgrounds of the members of our panel, I am impressed by what they bring here today. Sr. Mary Hennessey also served as director of formation for the members of her community. Fr. James Walsh was director of all the pastoral services for the Archdiocese of Cincinnati and consultant on adult education for the archdiocese. Fr. John Linnan served as assistant provincial of his own order, the Viatorians, and he has been in seminary education both as a professor and as a rector. Fr. John Strynkowski spent ten years in Rome in addition to his studies, a period in which he served in the Roman Curia in various capacities. I think these are all excellent credentials for contributing to our discussion today.

I would suggest that the focus of this panel is a very practical one: Who has responsibility for the education of laity in relation to ministry? And second: What is the role of theological seminaries?

The context of theological education in this country has changed dramatically in the past twenty-five years, not only in Roman Catholic seminaries but in others as well. The one privilege I have in my present position is that I regularly travel to some two hundred and ten seminaries. I am responsible for their accreditation; for the review of their programs; for the goals they are setting for themselves; and for how they are dealing with similar problems in their own denominations. And believe me, this cuts across the board in seminaries. The demands being made of them are changing rapidly because the way in which ministry is offered and the way in which people are prepared for ministry has been changing rapidly in the past twenty to twenty-five years.

It is only now that the schools see themselves as in a position to take the reins and really begin to respond to this with some sound planning. They have done the tough work of reviewing their financial resources and, by and large, are in a far better position in terms of planning than they were a decade ago, even though they don't have more money. The second stage is that of accommodating their programs to these demands. If you can anchor your resources, at least the financial resources, and begin to assess your personnel, then you can look at what's being asked of you and start designing and measuring the programs according to what you think you really can do in relation to your Church.

I have the responsibility of maintaining and developing the annual set of statistics on all theological seminaries in the United States and Canada. To give you one example of the change, at the present time, over twenty-six percent of the students in the theological seminaries in the United States are women. Catholic seminaries are not far behind that general average; the average there is about twenty-one percent. The average for faculty is thirteen to fourteen percent women, and I think our seminaries are a little behind that because the number has dropped since the Vatican studies. In fact, one of the effects of the Vatican study of seminaries was to make women feel unwelcome in our theological seminaries, which I think is unfortunate because they have made a substantial contribution to establishing the context in which we prepare people for ministry.

If you think the concept of change is a difficult one only for the Catholic Church, you have another thought coming. Recently, I spent several days at a large, conservative evangelical seminary in the Southwest. That school, in a strong dispensationalist tradition, admits onto its faculty and student bodies only those who will sign its Statement of Faith, and that signature has to be reaffirmed annually. This places severe restrictions on whom they can place on their faculties. They took heart and were, frankly, in great wonder of a change that was being exercised at a small Protestant church in their area. In front of that church was an illuminated sign and over a period of several months, that sign reflected these changing times. Initially, the pastor was announced as the Reverend John Neil, Pastor. A few weeks later it was Reverend John Neil, Pastor; Reverend Joan Neil, Assistant Pastor. Two weeks after that it was Reverend John Neil, Pastor; Reverend Joan Neil, Associate Pastor. Within a month, they were announced as co-pastors. And, yes, the next step did follow: Reverend Joan Neil, Pastor; Reverend John Neil, Associate Pastor. And then it was just the Reverend Joan Neil, Pastor.

Those at the evangelical seminary are, themselves, trying to face the need of change. They know it has to come, but it is a very painful thing. So, I think this experience is something we share with others—for better or for worse. But we can talk to other people, and that is the beauty of sharing. We can share our experience with them, and they can share their experience with us.

I have offered a brief context for our discussion, trying to establish a few of the questions.

Number one is the question of the need of providing education for laity for ministry. This is something the Church recognizes. If people are going to go out and assume responsibility for ministry, the Church has a responsibility, as a community, to offer them some preparation. This embraces not only the academic elements—they are the easiest—but also the formational aspects. The context in which preparation for ministry takes place is of critical importance. *Context* means the classroom; the worship experience; the contact with peers who are studying and preparing for ministry; the contact with teachers who represent the tradition; and an adequate amount of time to let everything sink in and mature. You see very few degrees by correspondence for ministry preparation that are worth anything in the public forum. You have to be with peers; you have to interact in order for some of this to take root.

The next question is, Who has the responsibility for preparing people for ministry? Theological seminaries are one very strong resource, but by no means the only one.

The third question goes back to a very common principle in education and accreditation. We send out visiting teams to these schools to ensure that no new program is instituted at the cost of other programs. If a school institutes a new program, it has to give evidence that it has the necessary resources, that the program is clearly thought out, and that it will not prejudice the quality of other programs.

Now enter the Congregation for Catholic Education, the Vatican study, and Bishop Marshall. Their statement is a very simple one: It appears that the integrity of the program for ordained priesthood has been prejudiced by new programs and by the presence of laity. And, they propose a simple solution: Separate that program from others. The question we are asking ourselves within the domain of theological education is: Have the programs of preparation for priesthood, in fact, been prejudiced by these changes? Is that a *fact* or is that an *assumption*? If, in some cases, these programs have been prejudiced, is what they are asking the real solution in light of our experience and in our context? Or would we be substituting one problem for another, which may well be worse than the first?

The presence of laity in the context of preparation for ordained ministry is a *reality* in this country. The change has taken place; they are there. It is really a question of more or less because that context has already changed. Second, the presence of programs for nonordained ministry is a reality. Sometimes they are academic programs for degrees, sometimes not; but they are there. The question of how to deal with this while preserving quality and, at the same time, relating it all to the Church is a real one. It's on the doorstep of most schools, and they know it. Schools are not reluctant to deal with laity; there are very few that have not already taken steps to address this question. But the question of what our position should be on a broad basis, that's open for discussion. We have much to learn.

I turn to my panel for their advice.

SR. HENNESSEY: Thank you, Monsignor, for providing some of the context. Now, I would like to delve a little deeper into what we might learn from looking at the broader picture of Christian education for ministry.

First of all, I think we need to face the fact that we share some major concerns with Protestants. For example, the relationship between laity and ordained clergy is a concern in all the Christian traditions. We see it especially coming to the fore because while we Catholics see ourselves in short supply, Protestants see themselves in oversupply and wonder why so many people should be ordained. Another concern is the place of professionality in ministry. I think the Roman Catholic community has, in fact, followed the Protestant community in accepting ministry as requiring professional training and preparation. That is quite different from the original, or the Orthodox, understanding of priesthood which is basically a "holy man." Now we have laity who are talking about "full-time ministry," which was one of the definitions used of clergy. They want to know what it means to be a professional lay minister. They want to know what standardizations are taking place, what qualifications will be required, and how they will be validated. A third mutual concern is that the best and the brightest men are not as frequently choosing ordained ministry—in any Christian tradition. Roman Catholics were slower than Protestants in catching up with that reality, and the newest community to face that situation is the black community. I think another part of that reality is that the most gifted and promising students in all seminaries tend to be women. In the Protestant community, they are ordaining women; in the Catholic community we are creating a new category for some of the women who are the most promising.

The second major point I want to make concerns another characteristic of seminaries today: interest in ministerial service for most candidates now follows some years of working in the secular world, pursuing other careers. That is true whether they are candidates for lay ministry or ordained ministry. Fewer seminarians are coming directly from college into ministerial training. Further, the background in religious understanding that could have been assumed in previous generations of candidates can no longer be assumed for either Protestant or Catholic seminary students.

The concern for formation, as opposed to theological education, is something that has surfaced very strongly for Protestant communities because of the advantages that they see evidenced in the Catholic seminary system. But that has happened at the very time that the whole question of formation in Roman Catholic education is under serious scrutiny. I think it is fair to say that before, formation meant literally what the word said: people were *formed;* they were provided with opportunities to exercise those things that would allow them to be the kind of people we wanted them to be. Now, we are constantly hearing about *education* in its root meaning, that is, something is being brought forth from the person. There is an awareness of the gifts given through baptism that are now seen as the foundation for the way in which a person will become prepared for ministry. Those are really two different understandings of what is supposed to be happening in the preparation of ministers.

Mrs. Mulligan's talk was a perfect example of the fact that experiential learning is being validated in a way it was not in previous generations. That wonderful tautology, a "lived experience," is becoming the major validation for authenticity. This has serious implications if we are talking about lay preparation by clerical or religious community figures. Yesterday, for instance, we heard that some men who were thirty-five years old and in the seminary had to go home to fulfill family obligations and, therefore, were not able—I think this was the phrase—"to take the pure spiritual atmosphere of the seminary." In the eyes of many people today, that is an invalid statement. For them, there is not the sense that escape or separation is "more spiritual" than relationship and responsibility; indeed, quite the contrary is true.

People wonder why Catholics are going to Protestant seminaries. Certainly, the issue is sometimes money, but I think there are three other aspects that are clues as to why people are going to non-Roman Catholic seminaries, and perhaps they provide help in seeing the special issues in the ministerial preparation of laity in the Church.

One aspect would be the issue of spirituality. No one in Protestant seminaries knows how to provide it well, but all of them are convinced that it is something that includes concern for sexuality, concern for relatedness in family responsibilities, and a sense that somehow the ministry that is being performed touches the kind of spirituality that is followed.

A second aspect, which I think is central, is that students want a place where they can have room to doubt and reject without feeling the pressure of orthodoxy. In our society, we are dealing with a world that is culturally so pluralistic that, unless we provide the opportunity during the formation period, the questions are going to come later on and will be much more difficult to address and answer.

The third aspect is the very pluralism of the community. Going back to the pedagogical principle that "it is *living* the experience that makes it valid," they want simply not to *learn* about other people but to *live* with them, to *hear* them express who they are and what their values are. We have to ask ourselves how seriously we are taking this larger environment. The reality is that by the turn of the century in the United States, the second largest religious community, after Christianity, will not be Judaism but Islam. How well are our seminaries facing that? At Harvard, we have the Center for the Study of World Religions. By way of example, one of the students came back from being a chaplain at a state university and said, "We have such a large group of Black Muslims. I would never have known how to work with them if I had not had the experience of dealing with Islam during my preparation."

Now, we can't do everything for everyone, but we do have to face the fact that there are dimensions of the world as it is today that are not present in seminary preparation and that some of those dimensions are going to be needed by many of our students. We have been talking about *the* "model" for seminaries. I hope we don't ever achieve *the* "model," but rather that we talk about many different ways of fulfilling the needs of being the full presence of the Church in the world.

FR. WALSH: My comments are based on my experience of being part of a ministry training center in a diocese. The real question for me comes down to the *mission* of the institution: Is the mission to train just priests, or to train all parish-staff level ministries? For example, part of my experience has been in seeing a development in parishes of one or perhaps two ordained ministers working with a group of other people who have responsibility for various dimensions of parish life. Certainly, the obvious one is religious education. But others are developing: family life ministry, network of care, liturgy, youth ministry. In other words, people are coming in and coordinating various aspects of parish life at that parish-staff level.

The answer to the question "Who has the responsibility for the education of the laity at the level of parish staff?" fits into that context. I believe that the shepherd does, that is, the one who is responsible for the quality of ministry at the parish-staff level, namely, the bishop. I see our responsibility—those of us who run seminaries and ministry training centers within a local church or diocese—as an extension of that ministry. So, the *mission* is not the mission of the seminary. If we define the seminary as "for the formation of priests," we are in a bind. All other ministry training will be by default.

I would like to suggest that perhaps we need to remind our bishops to look at their responsibility to provide ministry training for the people at the leadership level. I really think we have been able to do that in our diocese, and we have been supported. Not so much that the bishop has been in the vanguard, but rather, supporting from the rear. That helps us to develop some models that will serve the Church in the short-term future. I am not talking about the long-term, when some of the issues that Fr. Hussey talked about will have to be addressed. That's a different Church, and I am excited about the possibilities. But for the immediate future, if we call upon our bishops to provide ministry training at the parish-staff level, I think that might alter our concept of structuring.

In our ministry center we have a seminary. Within the broader umbrella of the institution, the mission of that seminary is strictly priestly formation because that is a distinct ministry. We have a whole other operation for the formation of lay ministers. But both types of formation are within this ministry center. As a result, we don't have the situation where three-fourths of the students are seminarians and one-fourth of them are laity. What we have is an institution where three-fourths of our students are laity, with one-fourth seminarians. Which I think more closely approximates what's happening in the parish.

Calling upon those who are responsible for the education of the laity to look at the whole picture—not just the education and formation of priests, but lay ministers at the parish-staff level—can really help to shape our institution. As a result, we can hire faculty for the whole operation, and we can have separately designed programs, which was one of Mrs. Mulligan's suggestions. In our ministry center, the whole lay ministry dimension is designed and administered by three lay women. And, there is a lot of room for creativity. They don't have many of the limitations that the seminary has from the larger Church. They are free to develop and that is life-giving and exciting to see.

So, for me, the issue is the mission of the institution, and we need to broaden that in the local Church and call the bishops to provide for that ministry training. But providing for the formation is not enough. There is also the responsibility to provide for the continuing education of those ministers. We do that for the priests in the diocese. We even have placement services for the priest. Why not diocesan placement services for those lay ministers who have moved to that professional level or parish-staff level?

When we look at ministry training at that parish-staff or professional level, another question arises: How are these people financed? In many dioceses, there are large endowments and bequests made for the training of priests. So, when a young man comes to our seminary from another diocese and we give the tuition, he's trained and formed at no expense to himself. Very often, the diocese is even able to give stipends for other expenses. At the same time, in the other division, which has the same expenses for credit hours, all of the laity's training is financed out-of-pocket. An increase in tuition works a tremendous hardship on those laity who started out as parish volunteers and now have progressed to the point where they are looking at the professional level. There is a tremendous financial gap, and I think that it will become more of an issue down the road. We are already experiencing it in our ministry center.

FR. LINNAN: I could not help but echo what Fr. Walsh just said about financing the ministerial education of lay people in the Church. For the last seven years, that has been my number one concern as president of the Catholic Theological Union. The Church needs, absolutely *needs* ministers. And many of those ministers are necessarily lay people. Now, if we need *professional* ministers, they need to be *professionally* trained. And I think the Church as a real responsibility to help finance that professional training of lay people for ministry. We have no scholarships at Catholic Theological Union for religious men or for seminarians. But we have managed to put together a very small fund to provide scholarships for lay people. It is barely a beginning, but it is such a crying need, and we think it is absolutely essential.

Now, I would like to make three comments.

First of all, I feel very positive about educating lay men and women for ecclesial ministry in seminaries and in schools of theology. My experience in the last ten years at Catholic Theological Union strongly suggests to me that—at least until something better comes along—seminaries and schools of theologies are fine places for lay men and women to prepare themselves for ecclesial ministry in the Church. Seminaries have the resources—faculty resources, library resources—that are tremendously expensive to duplicate. And, as we have heard on several occasions, those resources are in danger of significant diminishment in the next few years. Also, I think that seminaries and schools of theology have real experience in educating people for ministry. It is one thing to educate a theologian, to train somebody from the classroom. It is another to educate somebody for intelligent, serious, theologically based ministry to people. That requires a different set of resources. And seminaries have those resources and that experience. Then, there is this whole business of *collaboration*. In a mixed model, we are educating men who will be ordained and men and women who will not be ordained, but who will be of necessity collaborating in the same profession. By having them together in the seminary for four or five years, we heighten the possibility of inducing that kind of mentality on the part of both that is essential for effective collaboration.

Catholic Theological Union has about a hundred and sixty men preparing for priesthood and close to two hundred sisters and lay people; lay people, by far, are in the majority. And, it seems to work.

The second comment I would make is to confess to a certain amount of confusion—a confusion that perhaps permeates a lot of our discussions. For the last two days, we have talked about lay ministers and ordained priests. I am not quite sure we know *who* we are talking about. By way of example, last year I attended a pre-synod convocation of the laity in Chicago. Again and again I heard people stand up and say, "Please do not call people who are in full-time service to the Church lay ministers. Lay ministry is something different. Lay ministry is the action of members of the community in the life of the world. It is not preparing liturgies. It is not catechizing."

Another example: Two years ago, we hired a young man to be a professor of patristics. We had the choice of a layman or a priest, and because of the different qualifications of background, we chose the priest. A year or so later I was invited to the baptism of the priest's daughter—and it was the bishop who celebrated the baptism. Obviously, there's a trick here: He is a Ukrainian priest. But the question is, to what degree are we confusing life styles with ministerial functions in the Church? To what degree do we identify the lay person as married and assume that one cannot be an effective minister in the Church if one is married and has a family? I talk often about ecclesial ministry and ecclesial ministers, some of whom happen to be ordained. But I am not sure if we can talk intentionally or clearly about laity and the clergy anymore, unless we sort out the difference between life styles and ministerial functions in the Church.

My third and final comment is about formation. Formation is extremely complex. There is a whole range of personal and spiritual formation that every person has to have no matter what kind of work he or she is doing in the Church or in the world. In our particular situation as a school of theology, we don't have any direct responsibility for what you could call *formation*, other than those kinds of personal and spiritual formative activities that are necessary for anyone who is going to be a public minister in the Church, be that person ordained or not. But the point I would like to make, as an educator and as somebody concerned about schools, is that in all of our talk about formation, we are beginning to underestimate seriously and, therefore, neglect the formative impact of education itself.

What happens in the classroom is often more formative than what happens in a lot of other activities, and we have to be very careful not to neglect that. I have an expression—it is probably not true, but at least it helps me: We have to touch people's minds before we can move their hearts and shape their behaviors. If we don't touch their minds, the effect on their hearts and their behaviors will be temporary at best.

FR. STRYNKOWSKI: I would like to begin my remarks with an anecdote, a statistic, and a quotation.

The anecdote has to do with a teaching experience. We have an master of arts in theology program in which I teach ecclesiology. In that course, we spend a good amount of time going through the Vatican II documents. Once, about halfway through the term, one of the women raised her hand and, with a shaking voice, said, "Father, why were these documents kept secret from us? Why were they hidden from us?" A very interesting comment. And this was only about five years ago, well after the time of the Council.

The statistic: The Gregorian University is the premier university in Rome. In a recent publicity brochure, they boasted that twenty percent of their students are women—not too far from the statistic that Msgr. Baumgaertner mentioned before.

The quotation is from Pope John Paul II, who was speaking to a group of French bishops during their *ad limina* visit. He said to them, "Your chief responsibility as bishops today is to teach your priests a new style of ministry, by which I mean more and more collaboration with lay people." And then he went on to note that "this should be done not because there is a shortage of priests but because, by baptism and confirmation, lay people have a responsibility in the Church and in parishes." Then, toward the end of his remarks, he said, "This whole area of lay responsibility in the Church is an area that requires more daring and imagination." The Pope was issuing a challenge to bishops of local churches.

But where does this collaborative style begin? Do we wait until after ordination and expect that it's going to happen automatically? Or should we begin to encourage that collaborative style and spirit in the seminary? It seems to me that one of the benefits of seminarians and laity studying together in some courses is the very practical experience of collaboration and mutual respect. The Congregation for Catholic Education has felt that this can lead to a blurring of the distinction between ordained ministry and the ministries of lay people—the other form of ecclesial ministry. But as a matter of fact, our own experience has been that it does force the seminarians to think about what it means to be a priest in a collaborative style of ministry. We encourage them to pursue seriously the question: What is it that you will be offering that is distinct? Thus, they increase their theological reflection about priesthood, and, consequently, we find that the seminarians develop a clearer notion of what they are going to be doing as priests. Generally, when seminarians feel that the identities are blurred, it turns out that there are really other problems. For example, the seminarian may be afraid of working with women or there are other difficulties, but it is not because of a theological problem.

The seminary is an invaluable resource. Seminaries have some of the best trained theologians in the Church today. Can we, in justice, deny that competence to lay people? Our seminary is located in an area where there are about three and a half million Catholics. There is only one other department of theology in our area. Where will the lay people go? And would we be doing the right thing if we denied them the opportunity to benefit from highly qualified theologians?

One of the things I have come to appreciate more in the light of Mrs. Mulligan's paper is that we cannot do lay formation. I used to think that was simply because we didn't have time to do it. And that's been a frustration for us. We have discovered that as lay people pursue theology, it has tremendous ramifications for their faith, as well as ramifications for their family life. They suddenly find themselves less able to speak with their spouses; they no longer share the same language in regard to religious matters, and that creates some distance and tension. And yet, we have felt frustrated in not being able to help them. The basic reason was lack of time, or so I thought. But now I see that we don't have the competence in terms of lay formation. I am not quite sure who is competent, and that is something of a dilemma. Ultimately, I suppose, it has to be lay people themselves who must develop this competence and work with each other—a form of peer ministry. I realize now that we need to encourage and enable this in some way, but it is not something in which we can engage.

In conclusion, my overall experience is that working with lay people and inviting them to share in our theological enterprise have been tremendously beneficial for the seminarians and for the larger Church.

MSGR. BAUMGAERTNER: Thank you very much. I am glad we got a chance to review this dimension of the problem. Mrs. Mulligan, would you have any comments that you would like to add by way of response?

MRS. MULLIGAN: I would like to elaborate on Sr. Hennessey's comment about students wanting a place where they can doubt and question. Coming from the lay experience, I totally relate to that. When I look back and think of what, for me, were strong formative models within the parish experience, it was those kinds of environments where people could come and learn. The educational component was certainly a part of it, but there was also that freedom to say, "We didn't learn it that way"; or, "Why is this?" I find also that as a lay person in the seminary, many seminarians are coming in and asking me that same question. There again, I present a different kind of model to them, one that is still wresting with things. A priest model presents more of a "finished" product; lay people are allowed to appear less settled.

MSGR. BAUMGAERTNER: I will now open the discussion to anyone who would like to pursue these issues, with comments.

DR. LANGAN: In the dispensation under which we have lived for at least the last past millennium, one of the functions that came along with ordination was a certain control, you might say, of orthodoxy. The ideal was, that when the candidate was ordained and then came forward as that very visible representative of the Church on the local scene, the laity could presume—it wasn't always the case—a correctness in teaching on his part. One of the issues that's emerging out of this greater role played by non-ordained ministers, many of whom are now full-time professionals, is precisely that question of orthodox teaching.

My point is that in this whole process of ordained and non-ordained ministers, we have yet to build in any kind of—and I hate to use the word, but if you are going to have unity in the Church, the word has got to be there ultimately—*control*, or *licensing* let us say, so that a person with an inferior status can listen to a person with authority and realize that there is some ecclesial backing.

SR. HENNESSEY: Thank you. That is a different issue, and I would agree with you.

FR. LINNAN: I think it could be argued rather clearly that ordination itself began as a form of ecclesiastical certification, that this person is competent to minister in this community or in the Church's life. We sorely lack a reasonable and intelligent way of certifying those whom we do not ordain. Now, ideally, we ought to ordain them, but until that time, we do need some kind of serious, intelligent, and carefully designed method of certification. Lacking that at the present time, one of the elements in the education of men and women for ministry is the development of that sense of integrity that says you cannot be a professional minister, whether you are ordained or not—and this has to be addressed also to the ordination candidates—you cannot be professional in ministry unless you are going into a community to serve that community and accept the fundamental faith orientations of that community. I would be like somebody graduating from Harvard Medical School and then going out to practice some form of quackery. It just is not being professional.

MSGR. BAUMGAERTNER: I thank all of you very much.

MR. HOFHEINZ: A spectacular ending to an extremely exciting two days. When we began yesterday, I promised a walk through the forest, a trip through the terrain in theological education, a sparkling array of guides through that terrain. I think all of my promises were delivered. Dr. Butler, I now turn the program to you.

DR. BUTLER: Thank you. We have had a really outstanding discussion. We have heard many voices. We have learned how dramatic the changes in Catholic seminary education actually are. In addition to our researchers, we have heard directly from those having the difficult job of directing today's seminary. A prominent archbishop metaphorically likens your job to that of composing a symphony with different themes and movements, yet blending in such a way as to be part of one work. It is hoped that we have not brought any dissonance into your lives in the airing of all these different viewpoints on the mission of the important institutions which you lead.

As foundations and donors, we expect to encounter, along with you and the rest of the Church, a continuing debate about the future of Catholic seminary education in the years ahead. This will surely not be settled in any series of meetings or through any one set of guidelines. Yet, the insights that you have shared with us in the Catholic foundation and donor community have stimulated our interest in this field and provided us with directional change and have ably demonstrated the resources required in the future. Thank you.

ABOUT THE SPEAKERS

REV. MSGR. WILLIAM L. BAUMGAERTNER has served as associate director of the Association of Theological Schools in the United States and Canada since 1984. A priest of the Archdiocese of Saint Paul and Minneapolis, Msgr. Baumgaertner is the former executive director of the National Catholic Educational Association in Washington, D.C. and was rector/president of the St. Paul Seminary (Minnesota) for twelve years.

REV. GERALD L. BROWN, SS, is currently the provincial for the Society of St. Sulpice (Baltimore), a post he will hold until 1991. Formerly the rector/president of St. Joseph's College (Mt. View, California), Fr. Brown was ordained for the Archdiocese of San Francisco and for seminary ministry with the Sulpicians in 1964.

DR. FRANCIS J. BUTLER is president and chief executive officer of Foundations and Donors Interested in Catholic Activities, Inc. (FADICA), a post he has held since 1980. A native of Alexandria, Virginia, Dr. Butler earned a doctorate in sacred theology from The Catholic University of America and is the former director of the Office of Domestic Social Development of the United States Catholic Conference.

REV. JOSEPH L. CUNNINGHAM, rector/president of St. Vincent de Paul Regional Seminary (Boynton Beach, Florida), is a priest of the Diocese of Brooklyn with degrees from St. Mary's Seminary and University (Baltimore) and the University of Notre Dame. Fr. Cunningham currently serves on the Advisory Board of the Bioethics Institute of St. Francis Hospital, the Vocation Board of the Archdiocese of Miami, and the Board of Trustees of St. John Vianney College Seminary.

REV. VINCENT D. CUSHING, OFM, is president of Washington Theological Union (Silver Spring, Maryland) and the former president of the

Association of Theological Schools in the United States and Canada. Educated at The Catholic University of America, Holy Name College, St. Bonaventure University, and Fordham University, Fr. Cushing has served as chair of the Appalachian Ministries Educational Resource Center (AMERC) since 1985.

REV. CHARLES L. FROEHLE is rector/vice president of The Saint Paul Seminary School of Divinity of the College of St. Thomas (Minnesota). In addition, Fr. Froehle is currently a member of the Executive Committee of the National Catholic Educational Association's Seminary Department, president of the Midwest Association of Theological Schools, a member of the Archdiocesan Commission on Investment Ethics, and the chaplain of the Saint Paul Serra Club.

REV. THOMAS F. GLEESON, SJ, president of the Jesuit School of Theology at Berkeley, holds degrees from Georgetown University, Fordham University, Teachers College of Columbia University, and Woodstock College (Maryland). A native of Leavenworth, Kansas, Fr. Gleeson was rector of the Jesuit Community and assistant professor of education at St. Joseph's University in Philadelphia before coming to The Jesuit School of Theology in 1986.

REV. EUGENE HEMRICK, director of the Office of Research at the National Conference of Catholic Bishops/United States Catholic Conference, is the author of numerous studies on topics that include catechetics, permanent deacons, campus ministers, diocesan pastoral councils, and seminarians. A syndicated columnist for the National Catholic News Service, Fr. Hemrick's most recent work is entitled *Seminary Life and Visions of the Priesthood: A National Survey of Seminarians* (1988).

SR. MARY HENNESSEY, a member of the Religious of the Cenacle, a community whose main works are retreats, spiritual counseling, and religious education, is the director for ministerial studies and a member of the faculty at Harvard Divinity School. A graduate of Radcliffe College, Sr. Hennessey received her graduate degree in pastoral counseling from Loyola University (Chicago) and has done further graduate work at Fordham, The Catholic University of America, and Boston University.

MR. FRED L. HOFHEINZ is program director for religion at the Lilly Endowment, Inc., where he directs the grants programs in theological education and in a number of areas of research in American religion. Formerly the chaplain to Roman Catholic students at Wabash College and DePauw University, Mr. Hofheinz is currently a member of the Board of Directors of FADICA.

REV. M. EDMUND HUSSEY is a priest of the Archdiocese of Cincinnati and the pastor of St. Paul Church in Yellow Springs, Ohio. Formerly the archivist of the Archdiocese of Cincinnati, he obtained degrees from the Athenaeum of Ohio, Xavier University, and Fordham University. Fr. Hussey has held numerous teaching positions and has traveled extensively to facilitate study of classical archaeology, classical and early European history, and the Greek and Russian Orthodox Churches.

REV. CHARLES M. KAVANAGH is executive director of the National Catholic Educational Association's Seminary Department and editor of the NCEA publications *Seminary News* and *Seminaries in Dialogue*. A priest of the Archdiocese of New York, Fr. Kavanagh holds degrees from St. Joseph's Seminary (Dunwoodie, New York) and from the Pontifical North American College (Rome). He is a former member of the NCEA Executive Committee and has also served on the NCEA Board of Directors.

REV. JOHN E. LINNAN, CSV, a member of the Chicago Province of the Clerics of Saint Viator, is currently associate professor of doctrinal studies at Catholic Theological Union (Chicago), where he served as president from January 1981 until November 1987. Fr. Linnan holds degrees from Georgetown University and from The Catholic University of Louvain (Belgium). He taught at the Viatorian Seminary (Washington, D.C.) and the Washington Theological Union (Silver Spring, Maryland) before coming to Catholic Theological Union.

MRS. MARY PATRICIA MULLIGAN is assistant professor of pastoral theology, director of theological field education, and director of the master of divinity program at Pontifical College Josephinum School of Theology (Columbus, Ohio). Currently enrolled in the doctrinal program in systematic theology at Duquesne University (Pittsburgh), Mrs. Mulligan holds degrees from Carlow College (Pittsburgh), Duquesne University, and Pontifical College Josephinum.

MOST REV. THOMAS J. MURPHY, a Chicago native, is coadjutor archbishop of Seattle, a position that he has held since May 1987. Formerly bishop of the Diocese of Great Falls (Montana), Archbishop Murphy is presently chairman of the NCCB Committee on Priestly Life and Ministry; advisor for the NCCB Committee on Priestly Formation, which he chaired from 1981 to 1984; a member of the Bishops and College Presidents Committee; and a member of the Ad Hoc Committee for the 1990 Assembly of the NCCB.

REV. DAVID J. NYGREN, CM, is a teacher, consultant, and researcher on management and governance in theological schools, hospitals, and other nonprofit organizations. Serving on the faculties of Boston University and the Graduate Theological Union (Berkeley), Fr. Nygren is an associate of the Cheswick Consulting Center (Boston) and a research associate of the project on "The Futures of Catholic Seminaries," sponsored by the Lilly Endowment and the Weston School of Theology.

REV. JOHN E. RYBOLT, CM, is rector/president of St. Thomas Theological Seminary (Denver) and a member of the Midwest Province of the Congregation of the Mission (Vincentians). A native of Los Angeles, Fr. Rybolt holds degrees from DePaul University (Chicago), Harvard University, The Catholic University of America, Pontifical Biblical Institute (Rome), Saint Louis University, and De Andreis Institute of Theology (Lemont, Illinois).

SR. KATARINA SCHUTH, OSF, coordinator of the Lilly Endowment project on "The Futures of Catholic Seminaries," is director of planning and registrar at Weston School of Theology (Cambridge, Massachusetts). Author of the forthcoming *The Futures of Catholic Seminaries/Schools of Theology* and co-author of *Cooperation among Seminaries* (also forthcoming), Sr. Schuth holds degrees from the College of St. Teresa, Weston School of Theology, and Syracuse University.

REV. ROBERT N. SHERRY is a priest of the Diocese of Rockford (Illinois) and executive director for the Secretariats of the NCCB Committees on

Priestly Formation and Vocations. A graduate of St. Meinrad College (Indiana), St. Paul Seminary (Minnesota), Loyola University (Chicago), and St. Mary of the Lake Seminary (Mundelein, Illinois), Fr. Sherry served as director of vocations for the Rockford diocese from 1975 to 1982 and is the author and editor of many vocations resources and publications.

REV. MSGR. JOHN J. STRYNKOWSKI is rector of Immaculate Conception Seminary (Huntington, New York), where he served as professor of systematic theology from 1979 to 1985. Appointed Chaplain of His Holiness in March 1976, and Prelate of Honor in May 1986, Msgr. Strynkowski was ordained in Rome for the Diocese of Brooklyn and holds degrees from Cathedral College and Gregorian University.

REV. JAMES J. WALSH, a priest of the Archdiocese of Cincinnati, is rector/president of the Athenaeum of Ohio/Mt. St. Mary's Seminary of the West (Cincinnati). Formerly director of the Department of Pastoral Services for the archdiocese and adult education consultant for the Office of Religious Education, Fr. Walsh has coordinated parish renewal efforts in Cincinnati for the past ten years.

APPENDICES

117

Appendix I
Structural Models of Theologates

Appendix II
Profile of Enrollment in Theologates
Based on CARA Statistics

Appendix III
Faculty: Degrees and Vocational Status

Appendix IV
Summary of Major Findings of Four Studies

Appendix I

Structural Models of Theologates

I. FREE-STANDING SEMINARIES/SCHOOLS OF THEOLOGY

This type of school "provides the entire program of spiritual, intellectual, and pastoral formation/education" (PPF, p. 7). Within this broad category fall 30 schools, which can be further sub-divided on the basis of their mission as follows:

A. For Diocesan Priesthood Candidates

- Saint John's Seminary, CA (CM)
- Saint Patrick's Seminary, CA (SS)
- Mount Saint Mary's Seminary, MD (Diocesan)
- Saint John's Seminary, MA (Diocesan)
- Kenrick Seminary, MO (CM)

B. Diocesan and Religious Priesthood Candidates

- Saint Meinrad School of Theology, IN (OSB)
- Pope John XXIII National Seminary, MA (Diocesan)
- Pontifical College of Josephinum, OH (Diocesan)
- Sacred Heart School of Theology, WI (SCJ)

C. Diocesan Candidates with Separate Programs for Others

- Saint Mary of the Lake Seminary, IL (Diocesan)
- Saint Mary's Seminary and University, MD (SS)
- Saint Joseph's Seminary, NY (Diocesan)
- Saint Charles Borromeo Seminary, PA (Diocesan)

D. Diocesan Candidates and Lay Students

- Holy Apostles Seminary, CT (MSsA, changing to involve dioceses)
- Seminary of Saint Vincent De Paul, FL (Several dioceses)
- Saint John's Provincial Seminary, MI (Several dioceses, changing to one)
- SS. Cyril and Methodius Seminary, MI (Diocesan)

- Immaculate Conception, NJ (Diocesan)
- Christ the King Seminary, NY (OFM)
- Seminary of the Immaculate Conception, NY (Two dioceses)
- Mount Saint Mary's of the West, OH (Diocesan)
- Saint Mary Seminary, OH (Diocesan)
- Saint Francis Seminary, WI (Diocesan)

E. Religious Candidates and Other Students

- Maryknoll School of Theology, NY (MM)
- St. Anthony-on-the-Hudson, NY (OFM Conv.)

F. Diocesan, Religious, and Lay Students

- Saint Thomas Seminary, CO (CM)
- Notre Dame Seminary, LA (Diocesan)
- Mount Angel Seminary, OR (OSB)
- Saint Vincent Seminary, PA (OSB)
- Mary Immaculate Seminary, PA (CM)

II. SUPPLEMENTAL MODEL—UNIVERSITY-RELATED

This model is described in the PPF (p. 7), as one "which provides one or more parts of the program from its own resources while other parts (such as the academic) are provided by another institution (such as a university). This category covers all houses of formation, which do not have academic programs. Since this study is intended to examine all institutions that provide the academic programs for priesthood candidates, the houses of formation are not included, unless the students are enrolled in a university that would not otherwise be considered a theologate. For purposes of this study, these are listed under university-related programs. The houses of formation are not listed here, so as to avoid counting the students twice, once in their residence and once in the academic institution.

- The Catholic University of America, DC (Diocesan)
  (A large group of diocesan priesthood students come from Theological College, but also some from other houses of formation.)

- St. John's University, MN (OSB)
  (Priesthood students from St. Cloud Diocesan Seminary and from St. John's Abbey.)

- Moreau Seminary, IN (CSC)
  (Students attend University of Notre Dame)

- St. Paul Seminary, MN (Diocesan)
  (Seminary is part of School of Divinity, St. Thomas College)

- Aquinas Institute, MO (OP)
  (Students take some courses at St. Louis Univ.)

- Saint Mary's Seminary, TX (Diocesan)
  (Students attend St. Thomas University)

- Mater Dei Institute, WA (SJ)
  (Students attend Gonzaga University)

- Centro de Estudios Dominicos (CEDOC), PR (OP)
  (Affiliated with Bayamon University)

- The American College at Louvain, BEL (Diocesan)
  (Students attend Catholic University of Louvain)

- The North American College, Rome (Diocesan)
  (Students attend several universities)

III. COLLABORATIVE SCHOOLS

This model is described as one which "recognizes the sharing of resources in a different way for the formation and education of priests." Three expressions of the collaborative model are identified.

A. Union Model

- Catholic Theological Union, IL
- Washington Theological Union, MD

B. Federation Model

- Franciscan School of Theology, CA (OFM)
- Jesuit School of Theology at Berkeley, CA (SJ)
- Dominican School of Theology, CA (OP)
- Weston School of Theology, MA (SJ)
- Oblate School of Theology, TX (OMI)

C. Mixed Model

- Dominican House of Studies, DC (OP)
- Oblate College, DC (OMI)
- DeSales School of Theology, DC (OSFS)

IV. OTHER

- St. Gregory the Theologian Seminary, MA (Eparchy of Newton) Melkite Greek Catholic Seminary

- Byzantine Catholic Seminary of Saints Cyril and Methodius, PA (Byzantine Archdiocese)

Monastic Training

- Monastery of the Holy Spirit, GA (OCSO)

- St. Joseph's School of Theology and Institute of Monastic Studies, MA (OCSO)

Categories are based on descriptions from the *Program of Priestly Formation.*

Appendix II

Profile of Enrollment in Theologates Based on CARA Statistics

	1967–68	1975–76	1985–86	1986–87
Diocesan Priesthood Students	4,761	3,109	2,672	2,661
Religious Order Priesthood Students	3,211	1,594	1,217	1,170
Unaffiliated Priesthood Students	——	16	31	22
Nonordination Students: Full Time	——	479	2,328	2,459
Part Time	——	(1,089)	(526)	(508)
TOTAL	7,972	5,198	6,248	6,312
Less Nonordination	——	479	2,328	2,459
Priesthood Candidates	7,972	4,719	3,920	3,853
Proportion of Priesthood Candidates	7,972 100.0%	4,719 90.8%	3,920 62.7%	3,853 61.0%
to Nonordination Candidates in	None listed	479 9.2%	2,328 38.4%	2,459 38.0%
Seminaries/Schools of Theology	7,972 100.0%	5,198 100.0%	6,248 100.0%	6,312 100.0%

(continued on next page)

Notes: In 1966–67, the total number of priesthood candidates was 8,325. For every 100 priesthood candidates in 1966–67, there were:

96 priesthood candidates in 1968–69
57 priesthood candidates in 1975–76
47 priesthood candidates in 1985–86
46 priesthood candidates in 1986–87

When tabulating individual statistics, some variation in numbers occurs. The figures used here are the CARA summaries for 1967–68. The 1975–76 CARA summaries are incorrect due to double counting, so these figures are recounted to reflect the actual numbers. For the last two years, statistics are tabulated for each seminary. The summaries are not significantly different.

Appendix III

Faculty: Degrees and Vocational Status

	Diocesan	Men Rel.	Women Rel.	Lay Men	Lay Women	TOTAL
PHD	45	115	41	37	13	251
STD	81	111	2	6	1	201
DRS	13	31	1	15	1	61
JCD	15	17	1	1	1	35
DMIN	8	11	5	—	2	26
Doctorates	162	285	50	59	18	574
Percent	55.5%	72.7%	53.8%	67.0%	54.5%	63.9%
SSL*	12(4.1%)	19(4.8%)	—	—	—	3.5%
SSL & DOC	174	304	50	59	18	605
Percent	59.6%	77.6%	53.8%	67.0%	54.5%	67.4%

Licentiates, Masters, Bachelors

	Diocesan	Men Rel.	Women Rel.	Lay Men	Lay Women	TOTAL
STL	48	30	1	2	—	81
JCL	9	3	—	—	—	12
THM	4	4	1	—	—	9
MA	29	31	38	21	15	134
MDIV	26	19	2	3	—	50
BA	2	1	1	3	—	7
Total	118	88	43	29	15	293
Percent	40.4%	22.4%	46.2%	33.0%	45.5%	32.6%

Vocational Status:

by Number	292	392	93	88	33	898
by Percent	32.5%	43.7%	10.4%	9.8%	3.7%	100.1%

*SSL degrees are considered terminal teaching degrees by accrediting agencies and so are separately identified.

Appendix IV

Summary of Major Findings of Four Studies

We present here a few pages of principal findings from four recent studies of Catholic seminarians. All of the studies are less than three years old, and all contribute to an understanding of the present state of Catholic seminaries.

It may appear unusual that we include findings from four studies. We do it for the convenience of readers who want a brief overview of the findings of all the new studies. We could not include all of the findings but only those that seem important.

All of the statements below are taken from one of the four studies, and they are labeled to show their source. The four studies and their labels are *Seminarians of the Eighties: A National Survey*, by Raymond H. Potvin (labeled P), *Seminarians in Theology: A National Profile*, by Eugene F. Hemrick and Dean R. Hoge (labeled H1), The present study, also by Hemrick and Hoge (labeled H2), and *The Futures of Catholic Seminaries/ Schools of Theology*, by Sr. Katarina Schuth (labeled S).

Part I. Overall Profile of Seminarians

A. Basic Demographics

1. About three-fourths of the theologians are studying for the diocesan priesthood. The remaining theologians are studying for a religious order or community. (H1, H2)

2. The ages of seminarians fall into three categories almost equal in size: early to mid-twenties; mid-twenties to thirty; thirty-one and over. (H2)

3. The strongest nationalities of seminarians are found in the Irish and German (including Austrian, Dutch, and Swiss) categories. Hispanics, although growing in number of seminarians, are still greatly underrepresented. (H2)

4. The majority of seminarians today were born Catholics. Only 6 percent are converts to the Catholic religion. (H1)

5. The majority of seminarians spent most of their adolescent life in the East North Central, Middle Atlantic, and New England regions of this country. (H1)

B. Secular Experiences

6. Most seminarians have dated, but very few have been married or have children. Few have had military service. (H1)

7. Forty percent of the seminarians have had previous social service experience, with community work rating first, hospital work rating second, and social work rating third among the top three types of experience. (H2)

C. Family and Parish Stability

8. Most seminarians and their families have low residential mobility. The average stay in a parish and time living in one residence is seventeen years. (H1)

9. A little more than one-fourth of the seminarians have lived in a national parish. (H1)

D. Schooling

10. Forty-nine percent of today's theologians have attended Catholic schools for all of their elementary education. (H1)

11. Forty-seven percent have attended Catholic high schools for all of their secondary schooling. (H1)

12. Fifty-five percent of the seminarians have had four years or more of Catholic college. (H1)

13. Nine percent of the major seminarians have had four years of seminary high school training. (H1)

14. Thirty-three percent have had four or more years of seminary college training. (H1)

E. Financial Situation

15. Approximately one-fifth of the seminarians have difficulty paying for their seminary training. (H1)

16. Most seminarians rely on funds from their bishop or religious order. (H1)

Part II. Psychological Profile

17. Overall, seminarians in 1984 score better than seminarians in the past on psychological scales. (P)

18. The relationship with the father in 1984 is much the same as it was in 1966 with regard to strictness, affection, and supportiveness. The mother, however, is seen as closer to her son and more overprotective than in 1966. (P)

19. Seminarians today agonize less over decisions and are more ready to assume responsibility than in the past. (P)

20. Fewer seminarians today report discomfort with superiors and interpersonal inadequacy. (P)

21. Seminarians are not self-conscious and reticent with persons in authority. (P)

22. Seminarians in 1984 are more open-minded and score higher on morale than seminarians in 1966. (P)

Part III. Influences on Seminarians

A. Family Background

23. The median income of seminarians' families is comparable to the median income of all Catholics. (H1)

24. On the average, seminarians' parents are more educated than the parents of all Catholics aged 20–39. (H1)

25. Seminarians come from families similar in size to average Catholic families and most have both parents Catholic. (H1)

26. The parents of seminarians attend Mass regularly and are moderately involved in other church activities. (H1)

27. Exactly three-quarters of the seminarians have both parents alive and living together. (H1)

28. Three percent of the seminarians report that their father had once studied for the priesthood. (H1)

B. Influences on Vocation

29. Most seminarians first thought of becoming a priest in elementary school but did not make a definite decision until college or after college. (H1)

30. There has been a decline since 1966 in the number of seminarians who have relatives and close friends in the religious life.

31. Most seminarians were altar servers and have participated in retreats and vocational programs. (H1)

32. Vocation talks and literature have a moderate influence on men in deciding to become priests, but magazine ads and television ads have very little effect. (H1)

33. The two most influential factors causing seminarians to become priests are an inner calling and a priest's example. (H2)

34. Over half of the seminarians have been involved in parish services before entering the seminary. The most predominant services have been in the areas of education and liturgy. (H1, H2)

35. Approximately one-fifth of the seminarians have lived a month or more in a rectory or monastery before deciding to enter the seminary. (H1)

Part IV. Opinions and Visions of Seminarians

36. Seminarians in the 1980s are more traditional than twenty years earlier. They tend to stress the essential and unchanging aspects of Catholic doctrine. (P)

37. Seminarians see the primary task of the Church to be that of encouraging its members to live the Christian life rather than to try to reform the world. If present attitudes are any indication of the future, tomorrow's priests will be less "activist" than in the past. (P)

38. Compared with 1966, more seminarians in the 1980s stress that the role of the priest is a life-long commitment. The percentage of seminarians who see celibacy as a meaningful expression of dedication to Christ has increased since 1966. (P)

39. One-third of the seminarians would consider marrying if the Church would permit it. (P)

40. There is a significant minority for whom celibacy does not appear to have much meaning. (P)

41. When asked if they would welcome a greater role for minorities,

women, laity, permanent deacons, parish councils, and ecumenical activities, two-thirds or more of the seminarians report a need for expanding these roles. (H1)

42. Being prayerful is the most important quality seminarians point to for any religious ministry. Second is being able to relate to people. (H1)

43. Seminarians report that the most important activity in any religious ministry is building community, with preaching ranking second. (H1)

44. Holiness is seen as the most important quality a priest can possess, with apostolic zeal ranking a distant second. (H1)

45. Preaching and teaching are seen as the most important activities a priest can be involved in, with celebrating the sacraments following a close second. (H1)

46. Responsibility ranks first and apostolic zeal second as the most important qualities seminarians feel they need. (H1)

47. Being able to help people is what seminarians think they will like best in the priesthood. (H1)

Part V. Seminary Life and Attitudes toward Seminary Experiences

A. The Seminary and Those Who Make It Function

48. Seminary structures have changed dramatically over the last 20 years. Many seminaries have amalgamated; students have greater freedoms; psychological testing of candidates is employed; many seminarians study alongside nonseminarians; and they are accustomed to internships, field education, and a less rigid theological standardized manual approach to their studies. Also, many seminaries have begun to admit older students. (H2)

49. Students report that seminaries possess excellent personnel; they have well-conceived programs, and they have a keen awareness of the needs of the Church in America. (H2)

50. Most theologates are reexamining their mission statements and re-

defining or reaffirming their present mission. The reasons for these deliberations are the following:

a) Some are reaffirming their present mission of only preparing men for ordained ministry.
b) Others are responding to the need of lay people to prepare for ministry.
c) Some are maintaining a mixed model out of conviction that the most effective preparation for priesthood takes place in a school with a diverse student body.
d) And yet others are reviewing their mission because of impending accreditation, when visiting teams insist that each school be aware of its mission and of the programmatic implications. (S)

51. In 1966–67, some 8,916 seminarians were enrolled in about 130 theologates. Today, some 3,853 seminarians are studying theology in 54 schools, along with at least 3,000 full-time and part-time students who are not preparing for ordination. (S)

52. Fifty-three out of fifty-four rectors/presidents of seminaries assert that the changes having the most positive impact on the quality of programs for priestly formation are the admission of lay students and the hiring of a more diverse faculty, including women religious and lay men and women. (S)

53. Though theologates with a mixed student body are numerically in the majority, American bishops are most frequently choosing schools for their priesthood candidates that enroll only seminarians. (S)

54. The reasons given for advocating a seminary without lay students are (a) Priestly identity can best be acquired in a separate traditional milieu. (b) Courses and formation programs need to have a specific emphasis that is not possible when nonordination candidates are enrolled. (c) The best environment for training celibate future priests is one that is in isolation from nonordination ministry students. (d) Resources would be needed for expanded programs and student services, which many believe would lead to a dual-track system. (S)

55. The reasons given for advocating a seminary training that is mixed are (a) Priestly identity can be achieved and appropriated best when it is tested in the process of formation by interaction with nonpriesthood students. (b) Theologates should be on the cutting edge in

preparing people not only for priesthood, but also for different kinds of professional lay ministry. (S)

56. The role of rector has changed. Some 15 to 20 years ago the "administration" of seminaries was, in effect, the rector. Now there are business managers, academic deans, and a host of other administrators sharing the rector's role. In many seminaries, the rector has taken on new responsibilities: development and fund raising, recruiting, maintaining the reputation of the school with bishops and religious superiors, and being involved in cooperative efforts with national organizations, professional groups, and other seminaries. (S)

57. The present rectors/presidents included 27 who are men religious and 23 who are diocesan priests. Of these, exactly half are new in their positions in the last three years. (S)

58. At present, there are 898 full-time seminary faculty and hundreds more who are part time. The average number of faculty members per school is 18. (S)

59. Regarding vocational status, among the 8,898 faculty members, men religious make up the largest number, 44%. Diocesan priests are the second largest group, with 33%. Women religious number 10%, lay men 10%, and lay women 4%. The total number of those who are not priests but teaching full time in theologates is 24%. (S)

60. Most faculty members believe that being able to find and afford a faculty will become an increasingly acute problem. The reasons given are (a) The decrease in priestly vocations is making fewer teachers available. (b) Premier Catholic theologians are being attracted to Catholic graduate schools and secular universities where salaries and benefits are considerably higher. (c) Professors often take on many unwanted roles. (d) Motivation for doing scholarly work is low. (S)

B. *Present Perceptions of Seminarians about the Seminary*

61. There is a shift in seminarian's perceptions. Twenty years ago they saw their training as a broad professional formation. Now they see it as a spiritual formation for priestly life. (H2)

62. Most students think seminaries should include both priesthood candidates and the laity. (H2)

63. Seminarians feel less critical about their education than they did in 1966. They feel intellectual standards are reasonable, and guidance services, student-faculty relations, the liturgical life, and apostolic training rank very high. Most seminary instructors are perceived as current. (H2)

64. The greatest improvements over the twenty years were in "personnel and guidance services," "student-faculty relations," and "spiritual formation programs." (H2)

65. Most students feel that "elective courses," "internship in the apostolate," "intellectual autonomy," and "leadership opportunities" are very adequate in the seminary. (H2)

Part VI. Future Priestly Roles

66. Eighteen statements were given to seminarians and faculty members, aimed at learning what they felt were primary ideals to be lived in their priesthood. The 18 items were reduced to two common dimensions or ways of viewing priesthood. Both the seminarians and faculty members grouped the items the same way. The first dimension is termed "Institutional versus Communal Orientation." The institutional end is measured by:

    a) preserving the ecclesial and social structure of the Church;
    b) pastoring the Church through the transmission of doctrinal truths;
    c) being an extension of the bishop; and
    d) performing liturgical rites that are exclusive to the priesthood.

    The second dimension is termed "Social Leader versus Personal Witness Tendency." The social leader end is measured by:

    a) being an activist in getting the faithful to engage in issues such as poverty, racism, sexism, and pro-life;
    b) being in dialogue with the world in order to enhance constructive action and harmony within it; and
    c) being a moderator who coordinates ministry in the Church. (H2)

67. When asked what the primary focus of their priesthood should be, seminarians ranked highest "personal spirituality," "celebrating the sacraments," "giving homilies," and "ministering to the faithful." Ranked lowest were "administrating finances and parish or community facilities," "working with Charismatic groups, Cursillo movements and sodalities." (H2)

Part VII. Attitudes of Seminarians on Fewer Priests in the Future

68. When asked, "How do reports that predict fewer priests affect you?", the majority of seminarians said they feel encouraged to become priests by the reports. (H2)

69. When seminarians were asked, "Given the reality of fewer priests, how do you feel that will affect you in your future ministry?", just over half would encourage the laity to take over a larger number of functions traditionally assigned to priests. Over a third never referred to involving others, but rather expected to go it alone, taking on larger workloads. (H2)

Part VIII. Comparisons between Institutional and Communal Oriented Seminarians

70. Students stressing the institutional dimension of priesthood are more likely to go it alone, whereas those who stress the communal dimension are more likely to be collaborative with the laity. (H2)

71. Students with an institutional orientation and who go it alone tend to put greater stress on spiritual formation and less stress on practical ministry training. They also tend to recommend having only priesthood candidates in the seminary, and they rate their seminary higher than average on preparation for the celibate life and lower than average on opportunities to study at other institutions. They rate the following more important than do communal oriented seminarians: celebrating the sacraments, carrying out the goals of the bishop, visiting the sick and aged, making converts, encouraging vocations to the priesthood, communicating the teachings of the pope, and ministering sacred devotions. They are more encouraged to become priests by the impending priest shortage. (H2)

Part IX. Comparisons between Diocesan and Religious Seminarians

72. In thinking about their priestly futures, the diocesan seminarians tended to focus on the role of the priest in being an extension of the bishop, carrying out spiritual governance of the laity, and preserving the structures and authority of the Church, while the relig-

ious students more often emphasized collaboration with laity and enabling laity to carry out social ministries. (H2)

73. The religious seminarians are older, and fewer of them have attended college seminary. The religious seminarians are more in favor of a mixed student body in seminary (priesthood candidates and laity), and they report greater satisfaction with their seminary experiences. Views about future priestly roles are quite different in the two groups—mainly, the diocesan students tend to focus on the role of the priest in being an extension of the bishop, carrying out spiritual governance of the laity, and preserving the structures and authority of the Church, while the religious students more often emphasize collaboration with laity and enabling laity to carry out social ministries. (H2)